Flying
on the
Inside

A Memoir of Trauma and Recovery

Rachel
Gotto

Little
a

Published by Little A, New York

www.apub.com

Amazon, the Amazon logo, and Little A are trademarks of Amazon.com, Inc.,
or its affiliates.

ISBN-13: 9781542028738
ISBN-10: 1542028736

Cover design by Sarah Whittaker

Printed and bound by CPI Group (UK) Ltd, Croydon, CR0 4YY

Flying
on the
Inside

For Nicola and for Mum.

Introduction

The seed for the writing of this book was planted many years ago, at a time when I was so very ill and unable to fend for myself. It was put down at a moment when my life was quite literally at one of its darkest points, a time when I wondered if I would ever live a life of purpose or meaning ever again. And it was my lovely mother who set that first kernel of an idea that I might one day tell my story to the world. From where I lay at that moment my future looked bleak, and I questioned what life had left to offer me, now that I had lost pretty much everything I held dear. I'm not sure, to this day, if my mother really believed what she said at that time or whether it was just a way to offer me some distraction from my dire circumstances, but on one of the days when I was at my lowest, I remember her quietly saying to me that I would recover and that one day I would write about what had happened to me. A mother's desperate wish for her daughter, I would have said at the time! I can still recall the anger I felt when she spoke those words. I lashed out at her; I was furious at what seemed like a stupid notion, an absurd idea that, to me, only served to highlight the plight I was in. I could hardly move a limb at that juncture and I was fierce in my protest that no one would ever want to read about something so miserable, and I meant what I said. And there the seed remained, dormant, for almost another decade, until I began my work as a therapist. The clients who come to see me have mostly lived extremely challenging lives themselves and often it's difficult for them to envisage the possibility of change, such is the depth of their experiences. Often, they have no concept that life can be different, and they feel completely stuck. Over time I found I could bring shifts in their perspectives by offering insights from my own journey, and soon I began to get referrals by virtue of my own story of trauma and recovery, and it was here that the idea of writing a book about my life began to be nurtured. Clients would time and time again choose to work with me because they'd heard that I too had experience of deep personal trauma and, as a consequence, they felt better able to trust me with their own struggles. Word of mouth landed me with an invitation to speak on the radio and that interview resulted in a flood of requests to hear more about my life. People were curious; they wanted to know how I had got from trauma to full recovery, and it was sometime around this point that I was prompted to seriously consider the idea of putting pen to paper. I won't lie, it was daunting. I'd never written very much, apart from poetry and a diary. However, setting down my story in a formal sense became the most natural direction to take, and so I began.

This hasn't been a straightforward book to write. It hasn't been easy to open up emotional boxes that I had, in the intervening years, carefully sorted through and gently put away. Needing to capture the immediacy of some of the most turbulent experiences of my past has in truth been most difficult. On each foray back into the past I had to dig very deep and, at the same time, hold the trust that I had developed enough fortitude and strength through my recovery to withstand the pitch of emotion that came with this backwards journey. Reviewing those times in order to faithfully recount them felt deeply risky and required me to trust in my own level of healing. There were days when I was less robust and I felt the rising fear that I might get sucked into being retraumatised with no way back out. On those days I walked away, returning only when it felt emotionally safe to do so. I took care of myself as best I could in the process, but, of course, there were many tears shed and, possibly, the most difficult aspect was that, having gone there again emotionally, I had to consciously and carefully repackage my emotions and put them back in the place I'd strived so hard to get them to, after so many years of therapy and processing. Nevertheless, I'm so proud that I was able to do this work. My mental strength has been tested in the recounting of this story, but mostly I'm happy to report that the whole experience has ended up feeling very cathartic.

Writing this book has definitely completed another layer of healing within me and I feel even further recovered. So much so that, very recently, I took a pilgrimage of sorts back to the village and surrounds where this whole story is set: at Glandore Harbour, on the coast of West Cork in Ireland. I'd not been back to visit for some years, and I was curious about how I would feel, having packed up and left in haste all those years ago, primarily to put some distance between myself and the painful memories held there. The journey was easier than I expected, and I was pleasantly surprised at how joyous I felt as I once again laid eyes on my childhood village. I was able to see it differently this time. The old dread that I'd experienced on previous visits was transformed into wonderment at the sheer beauty of the area. In that moment I could understand why my parents had initially fallen in love with the place. As I stood once again on the shores of this remarkably beautiful harbour I felt that somehow I'd come full circle. The peaceful state I experienced in my body was new. The dark sense of loss and longing, as before, seemed all but gone, and as I stood looking out to where Adam and Eve Islands stand, iconic markers protecting the entrance to the waters of my childhood playground, I felt transformed. Checking in on myself, I looked across the bay to Union

Hall, the place where my late husband and I moored our boat, and the pier that we worked from. I saw the changes that had occurred in the years of my absence, and I was happy. It's difficult to put into words what I felt: a maturity, a sense of having come through a storm into calmer seas, with my sails set for a new destination.

The sea has always been part of my life, my one anchoring point in the emotional wilderness of childhood; one I often had to navigate alone. My brothers, too, all found connection there, with each of my three older brothers, Mel, Nicky and Adrian, later embarking on careers connected to the sea. In the same way, my brother Dominic, barely a year older than me and my constant childhood companion, left home at eighteen to become a transatlantic skipper, delivering yachts for clients between the Mediterranean and the Caribbean.

When, in my early twenties, I returned to the family home after years of escape in Dublin and then England, it was the sea that brought me my husband. Nic was an adventurer, a fisherman and a deep-sea diver, who at the time I met him was conducting marine research for University College Cork. With Nic, my own passion for the ocean flourished again, and deepened, when he taught me to dive. It was thanks to Nic that I discovered the silent, meditative world of the ocean bed, where I so quickly felt attuned, safe and, for once, completely at one with my environment.

Just as I was finding happiness with Nic, Dominic, by then in his mid-twenties, decided to return to Ireland for a bit, to take stock and see where the next escapade might take him. But the next – and final – journey that life held in store for Dominic was the very last thing any of us would have wanted for him. Two years later, at the age of twenty-eight, he was dead.

And it was the sea that took Nic from me, barely eight months after we were married, when I was pregnant with our first child.

In the dark years after Nic's death, I returned to the sea when I could. I swam; I listened to the wash of waves on long, sleepless nights; I walked endlessly along beaches.

Adapting to being not just a first-time mother but also a sole parent was an experience I shouldered with enormous difficulty. With my senses blunted from shock and grief, my ability to bond with my small baby in the early stages was all but dead. I struggled to comfort my fragile, fractious and already traumatised little girl and my own exhaustion was such that I was constantly teetering on the edge of a complete breakdown. Yet I just had to keep going. I knew I had love for Nicola, but I was so profoundly miserable when she was born that I had little to give. I desperately wanted to be alone; to be left to live with my pain. Thankfully, motherly instinct meant I managed most of the basics of her care, but I'm ashamed to say that she could have been someone else's baby in the early days, such was the extent of my emotional disconnect. The guilt was enormous; I tried so hard but failed to find the link that I somehow knew should be there. She cried so much, day and night, and I dreaded her mewling because its pitch would bite into my brittle reserve, and as she signalled her own pain to the world I howled with her. We were a sorry pair.

At just a month old, a red scratch mark that had been on her left eyelid since birth suddenly ballooned into a massive liverish lesion. Not knowing what it was, I immediately blamed myself. I thought I'd somehow caused this, that I'd injured her in some way. It was some relief to learn that it was a strawberry nevus, a haemangioma, a congenital form of birthmark, but I couldn't help but wonder if trauma in utero had brought it on. Doctors began treatment in earnest as they feared, if her eye wasn't able to open fully, Nicola wouldn't develop the sight in that eye. There were hurried trips to the capital city, Dublin, to see paediatric ophthalmic specialists; so many opinions were sought, and the wisdom at the time was that a medication-based approach would be safest, as the lesion was extremely vascular and surgery posed too much of a risk. Together we were caught up in an endless round of treatments and travel. However, something positive began to emerge at this point. I began to be fiercely protective of Nicola. I had always been medically very well informed, and this meant I could really watch out for her in a practical sense. I questioned doctors, I researched her condition, and through this something began to melt in my emotional wall. In effect, I began to feel something other than duty towards my little girl. A bond was beginning to form.

Nicola, sadly, despite all the medical help she received, lost almost all the sight in her left eye. Not that this ever affected her or impeded her life very much – the principle of not missing what you've never had applied. She grew into a robust little girl, with a wild streak for adventure and fun, and I had begun to love her fiercely.

During the time I was trekking up and down the country with Nicola, meeting with various specialists and seeking to maximise the chances of saving her sight, another story was unfolding at the house in Glandore where my mum lived. My eighty-nine-year-old father, who had remained paralysed and in bed following a stroke over six years before, had begun to lose his tight grip on life. For reasons that will become clear, I won't go into detail about my relationship with this complex and deeply troubled man here. But what I will say is that I hardly knew my father in reality. I didn't like him, and I had kept away from him as much as possible for much of my adult life. But in his final days I felt compelled to visit him again and, seeing him so frail and vulnerable, I couldn't help but feel a compassion of sorts. I was slightly surprised at this; I'd had very little do with him during his incarceration, but, nevertheless, I was drawn to be close to him at this point. In his final days, as I sat in silence by his side and listened to his changing breath, I wondered, in those moments, what his own childhood had been like and what he could have experienced himself to turn him into the dysfunctional father that he had been to me. He never spoke to me from his deathbed. I didn't say much to him. My last visits to him were mostly dutiful, but, strangely, I felt something of a slight warmth towards him as he passed on. I couldn't identify what it was precisely, but it was definitely peaceful in nature. Maybe it was, in those last few moments, as he lay in the space between this world and the next, that we reconnected in essence, as father and daughter once again. Who knows? My father died on 21 July 1999: an era ended, and I wasn't sad.

Eventually, I dived again. But just a few days later, Nicola found me unconscious on our kitchen floor. I was rushed to hospital, where a battery of scans and tests would reveal that I had a growth in my brain. I was told that at any moment – no one knew when – the mass could rupture and cause catastrophic injury to my brain, if not immediate death. I was told to make a will, and any other necessary preparations for my death, as soon as possible.

It was then that I had to give up scuba diving for ever; the soundless world of the ocean bed was no longer available to me. After an exhausting search for a surgeon who would be prepared to operate on my brain in spite of the risks, I had successful surgery to remove the tumour. My recovery from the resulting paralysis and the trauma of brain damage was to be agonisingly slow.

For the decade after my surgery, when I was kept on maintenance doses of a complex cocktail of drugs to keep my brain seizure-free and as quiet as possible, my physical and mental energy were so tamped down, so bludgeoned into a flat line, that I had no desire even to swim. I all but forgot my love of the sea and adventure. There was simply no energy for it. This was especially true of the two and a half years it took to wean myself off the most insidious of these drugs – the 'benzos'. That was a special kind of hell all its own, one that took me far from the essence of who I was and into a world of isolation, of strange visions, waking nightmares, thoughts of death, and worse, as I struggled to rid my system of these powerful chemicals.

When I was originally prescribed these drugs, I had no awareness of their potentially damaging effects on my quality of life – and to be fair, in all likelihood, neither did my doctors. In writing about this period of my life, I'm not seeking to blame the medics who were supervising my care. But I am trying to raise greater public awareness of this issue so that in the future others can make more informed choices about their health care.

Today, after over a decade in recovery – from the effects of my surgery and my physical dependence on those drugs – I can at last find solace in the sea once more. And I have found love again, with my wonderful partner of seven years, Malcolm. Together we spend weekends on Inishbofin Island, just six miles from the Connemara coast: fishing for mackerel, rowing between the islands, swimming and snorkelling off the rocks and walking along the beaches.

Malcolm, too, has had a hand in the creation of this book. He endlessly encouraged me to keep going when I fell into overwhelm, both at the monumental task of getting the story down and also when I became unravelled by the experience of emotionally revisiting my traumas in order to recount them. His finest role to my mind, though, has been that he came up with the title for this book. I had been musing for months about what the story should be called. There had been many suggestions but nothing that stuck, and, finally, I came down to breakfast one bright Saturday morning to find a lined A4 piece of paper on the table that read *Flying on the Inside by Rachel Gotto*. I loved it immediately, it was like a hand fitting a glove; in those few words he had cleverly encompassed my whole life story to date – and so, the title of this memoir was born.

The isolation I once felt so acutely is no longer a feature of my life. Today, I recognise that, like all of us, I am part of the community of people who share this planet. It's my right – and privilege – to live life to the full, and in a way that expresses everything that is good about our shared humanity: respect, creativity, compassion, kindness, connection. In writing this book, I hope to provide a way-marker of sorts for anyone who feels alone or who can't see or navigate a way forward.

Thank you for choosing to read this book. I feel deeply honoured that my story is worthy of your precious time, and it is my hope that when you come to finish the last page you will be left feeling uplifted and with a renewed zest for life.

Galway, Ireland
November 2020

Author's Note

I have chosen to write this book mainly about my own life, and not about my family. This is because I wish to honour the feelings of those still living and to afford them privacy. As a result, there are some obvious omissions, but these don't affect the heart of the story.

I've done my best to ensure accuracy of detail in this book but, brain injury being what it is, some of my memories and recollection of dates and actual events are not as precise as I'd like them to be. Some names and some geographical locations have been changed to protect the privacy of others.

One

Viking; North Utsire; South Utsire; Forties; Cromarty; Forth; Tyne; Dogger; Fisher; German Bight; Humber; Thames; Dover; Wight; Portland; Plymouth; Biscay; Trafalgar; FitzRoy; Sole; Lundy; Fastnet; Irish Sea; Shannon; Rockall; Malin; Hebrides; Bailey; Fair Isle; Faeroes; Southeast Iceland . . .

Throughout my turbulent childhood the one constant was the BBC World Service Shipping Forecast. Every evening, just before 6 p.m., my father would turn on the old Grundig radio, and after the six pips of the Greenwich time signal, the steady incantation of the thirty-one sea areas would resound in the kitchen.

I knew the names and the order in which they were read by heart: to this day, I can recite them fluently. Strange names that spoke to me of a wider world, one of open oceans and the possibility of perhaps one day getting to know some of these exotic-sounding places. Reassuring in their monotony, their unchanging sequence, they became something for me and my closest brother, Dominic, to cling to during the many difficult times at The Pier House on the shores of West Cork, which for many years was the family home.

The sea was a constant in the life of our family. So many of our activities, work and leisure were based around her: we swam, we sailed, we made our living in her waters – fishing, and later, when my parents set up their chandlery business, providing equipment to local fishermen and sailors. We were out of our element in the tiny beautiful shoreside village of Glandore in every sense of the word, but the sea was our saviour and in the ocean we all felt some sense of belonging. We were English; we had our own ways of thinking and living, and they were very much at odds with those of everyone else in the locality. In the Ireland of the late 1960s, we were blow-ins – quite literally.

In 1965 my father, Eugene Moses Bendon, and my mother, Shirley, had decided that they would sell up the family home in Leeds, Yorkshire, buy a large old wooden boat and equip it with the fittings of the house, including the coal-fired Aga from the kitchen and the living-room furniture. The intention was to sail the entire family to New Zealand on a grand adventure. My mother was twenty-five years younger than my father and they already had three young children – my brothers Mel, Adrian and Nicky, whose ages at the time were ten, eight and three respectively. Dominic and I were not yet born.

My father was not a born sailor; he didn't have much experience of boats and sailing, let alone the knowledge and skills needed to skipper a leaky craft across treacherous transatlantic waters to New Zealand, with no crew other than his equally inexperienced wife and three young sons. It was to be an adventure, and, sailing experience notwithstanding, they were off. If anyone had expressed any concerns at his abilities, they would have been dismissed immediately. He had no fear. He knew what he was doing, so he said, and my mother trusted him implicitly.

But they didn't get very far. My father had a few years previously bought a potato farm in West Cork and the plan was to first visit there to work on that year's harvest and then set sail. In late summer 1967, however, my mother found out that she was pregnant with Dominic and so their departure from Ireland was delayed. One year ran into another and then I appeared, and thankfully we didn't ever depart for the high seas. When I was born, in

May 1969, our boat was still moored in Glandore Harbour and the family mostly lived ashore in The Pier House, which my father had bought some time earlier on one of his jaunts. The only reason Dominic and I weren't born on board *Johanna* was because when my mother went into labour the doctor refused to oversee a birth on a boat, so she had us both at The Pier House.

When I was five, *Johanna* sank at Glandore pier in a storm. She was never repaired and finished her days rotting on the shore, high up the Leap estuary. And there we stayed, in West Cork, for many decades to come; those of us who survive still have strong ties to the area to this day. Just as he had decided on a whim to take his young family to the other side of the world, so my father concluded that we should simply stay put, where the ocean had taken us, in Ireland.

And since there was a large gap in age between us and our three older brothers, it was inevitable, I suppose, that Dominic and I were thrown together for most of our time from our earliest days. As young children we were inseparable – all the more so since, at the tiny village school where we spent our primary years, we were put into the same class, seated next to each other and felt very different from the other children. It was difficult to forget that we were different: we were still blow-ins, we were not Catholic, we didn't attend any church, we'd arrived on a boat, we ate home-made brown yeast bread, we sounded different. We were not made to feel different especially, we just were.

And this meant that we spent much of our free time alone together. In some respects, our childhood was idyllic – we had so much freedom, especially in comparison to the organised and safe existences afforded to some children today. Quite literally, all we needed to do was cross the road and we were at the sea. We spent hours of every day climbing the rocky shore, exploring every nook and cranny, and once we were old enough, and when the weather was right, we'd jump into our little blue-and-white rowboat and explore the length and breadth of the harbour. From the ages of five and six we were adept at catching our own food. I prided myself on being able to expertly break the fishes' necks by hooking my little finger into their mouths and pulling backwards until the fish was dead. Only I did that; Dominic didn't do that job! Nearly every morning began with us being laced into bright-orange life jackets, and off we would go, our day spent in comfortable companionship. Dominic, because he was older, was generally the boss. Most of the day's decisions were made by him, and that suited me; I looked up to him enormously. And this is how life continued for most of our young years.

When our older brothers had all left home – by which time I was twelve and Dominic thirteen – my parents moved to another house. I can still remember the excitement of what seemed to be a great development. My mother had long wanted to move; she disliked the lack of privacy that living at The Pier House entailed and she was deeply unhappy in her marriage. I guess she naively thought that a house move might somehow, miraculously, improve the fractious relationship she had with my father. I hoped this too. I didn't live in a happy home, and I also thought the move might in some way change all our lives for the better. I couldn't have been more wrong.

It was then that my father, who had always been a difficult man, seemed to become more driven than ever by his own demons, and since we were the only two children left living at home, Dominic and I often found ourselves at the sharp end of his torment. We were getting older, and his need to control us, especially Dominic, was becoming more pronounced. The longed-for move proved to be the beginning of some of the most emotionally trying times for each of us as my father spilled his frustration and anger on to us. In this new home, 'the big house', as we called it, we were more

16

isolated than ever before, not only from our peers, but also from society in general. The only saving grace was that the house was enormous, and once my father had settled into his evening routine of wine and opera we could hurriedly escape to our rooms and hope that he would leave us to our own devices until the next day.

From the earliest days of my childhood, my father repeatedly told me and my siblings that life had no meaning, that there is no God. Religion and other forms of spirituality were a nonsense ('poppycock' was his favourite word to express his contempt), something that only very stupid people could possibly subscribe to. It was a bleak view of human existence, but even as a small child it was one that at some instinctive level I rejected. Dominic and I were sent to a local primary school, under the auspices of the local Catholic Church. Because we were so close in age, we were put into the same class, and because we were not Catholic, we sat apart from the other children at times of religious instruction. This physical separation marked out, for everyone to see, the extent to which we were outsiders: 'others' who didn't fully belong. In the everyday life of the classroom, as in all such schools at the time, there were quite a few references to the Catholic religion and ethos – to prayers and Mass, to the Virgin Mary and the rite of Confession – and I remember, even at six years old, truly envying my classmates, that they had this other dimension to life and a belief in something beyond our immediate human experience. Theirs was an intriguing, enigmatic faith that there is another level of meaning to the world. I was captivated by the beauty of songs such as 'Ave Maria' and, at Christmas, the carol 'Silent Night', which inspired a deep, unfathomable sense of longing in me – something I can now recognise as a spiritual thirst. For me, these songs, as well as the sacred rituals of the Catholic religion, encapsulated my own sense that there was indeed something more to life, and that I somehow longed for this. But I never spoke of such things at home, especially in my father's presence, because I feared being ridiculed.

In so many ways, my childhood and adolescent years were difficult. I do, however, maintain that it was those same difficult experiences that armed me with a resilience and tenacity of spirit I might not otherwise have developed. The knowledge I gained from a young age about survival at sea and using my wits to get by equipped me with a vast array of resources and built the foundations of a personality that could withstand the deeply challenging events that were to come my way later in life.

Two

2005

I looked at the imaging of my brain on the black-and-white screen positioned at the foot of my bed. Even I, still stunned in the aftermath of the massive *grand mal* seizure that had left me passed out on the kitchen floor and without much medical knowledge of the brain, could see the dark, shadowy mass at the right-hand side of my skull.

I peered at the screen, trying to understand what they were focusing on. 'What is *that*?' I asked the consultant, who had supervised a student doctor as she'd inexpertly fed a line into my groin and along the artery running up into my head, then injected a dye (radio-opaque contrast agent, I learned) into it and watched its trajectory into my brain on the screen.

We were in the same theatre I'd been referred to in the flurry of activity that followed my arrival in Accident & Emergency. There had been an unbearably long silence as the two gazed at the screen.

'It seems, Rachel, that you have a very large lesion here' – he pointed – 'what looks like an AVM, in the right-frontal cortex. We'll have to do a lot more tests, but my sense at the moment is that, because of the size and location of the growth, treatment will be complex.'

I didn't know how to respond. I'd no idea what an AVM was and, in any case, the overwhelming fatigue that engulfed my body and brain made it almost impossible to formulate any further questions.

The next day, once further tests had been done and with my mother at my side, the same consultant returned to update us on their findings.

'We've had a good look and at this point are pretty clear about your situation. What you have, Rachel, is an AVM in your brain. An AVM, or Arteriovenous Malformation, is an abnormal growth of tissue which over time has developed its own system of blood vessels, of arteries and veins, and it's kind of operating independently of the body's normal circulatory system. These AVMs tend to be congenital. Yours was likely present from birth and has grown and developed until it has impacted, like they generally do, on the body's normal functioning. It's often in pregnancy that they make their presence felt first. Generally, they are benign – which, we are pretty sure, this one is – so, while they continue to grow, they are not often cancerous. That is the good news.

'The bad news is that this AVM is incredibly large – certainly one of the biggest I've seen in a while. AVMs are graded from one to six and, unfortunately, yours is looking like a six. It's very complex and this one is very developed – a large lesion. It's now completely enmeshed in the brain tissue, so surgery looks more or less impossible. It's also located in the right-frontal cortex, the motor centre for the left-hand side of the body. So, even if surgery could be done without extensive damage to the brain tissue, paralysis on the left-hand side of your body would be an almost inevitable consequence—'

He broke off for a moment, sighing. There was a long silence. None of us knew what to say. My immediate response was denial and a feeling that the doctor was exaggerating. The whole thing seemed absurd; I almost wanted to laugh. My mother was silent.

'So, is this why I've been having those weird experiences recently—' I began. I thought back to only the other day, when I couldn't get my hand to reach for the gearstick in my car; it simply wouldn't do what I wanted it to.

'Yes, the scans confirm that you may have also had a series of TIAs, mini-strokes – probably going back quite some time now, I'd say. That's why you've been experiencing loss of motor function in your left arm and your leg. When your daughter found you unconscious, you'd just experienced a major seizure. This often starts to happen as the tumour begins to make itself known. I'm surprised you didn't go to your doctor sooner,' he concluded, looking directly at me. I heard the disbelief in his voice; it was the last thing I needed.

'So, what's next?' I was finally able to ask.

'Ah, well . . . We've probably given you and your mum more than enough to think about for now,' he replied, looking uncomfortable. 'We can discuss all that at a later point. For now, I can tell you that I'm letting you go home tomorrow or the day after, and before you go, as soon as possible in fact, we'll get you started on Epilim – an anti-seizure drug used very successfully in epileptics. We'll be monitoring you on that as an outpatient, to see how you get on. As I said, surgery or any other kind of invasive treatment doesn't look very possible at this point, but you should certainly seek another opinion.'

Although I felt a shard of fear cut through me, I wasn't really able to take on board what this really signified or to connect with anything I might be feeling. We asked a few more questions, but I couldn't focus on the answers or on his responses. And then he left. A few minutes later, a nurse came in to administer a 'loading dose' of Epilim via an IV line – a very high starting dose designed to calm my brain and help prevent further seizures in the immediate term. Alone now, I sank back into the pillow. With my brain blasted by the earlier seizure and as the Epilim began to take its bludgeoning effect, I welcomed the respite from awareness, no matter how brief.

Late the next afternoon, my gorgeous friend Breeda arrived on the ward, but while she had her usual cheery energy, she also looked concerned. I knew she'd been in touch with my mum after a further session with the consultant that morning, when he'd shared more thoughts about my possible prognosis. He'd again been clear that, in his opinion, any aggressive medical intervention – surgery, chemo, radiotherapy – appeared not to be a viable option. The best way forward was to find the right cocktail of medication to strike the balance between keeping my brain stable and any side effects minimal. If the dosages were too low, my risk of suffering further, devastating seizures would increase; too high, and I'd be left feeling permanently lethargic and emotionally blunted. Getting the most beneficial doses would involve a process of trial and error over the next few months. However, the bottom line was that the AVM would continue to grow unchecked and that in all likelihood at some point I'd suffer a brain aneurysm and, ultimately, a fatal haemorrhage. When asked to put some kind of timeframe on it, the consultant said that it was difficult to say but I probably had about two years at most, but that it might well happen before then. At this point he gently suggested that it may be a prudent move to begin putting my affairs in order, to write my will and begin making necessary decisions about Nicola's future, should the worst happen soon than later.

Since that conversation and with Breeda's arrival, it was slowly beginning to dawn on me – through the haze of exhaustion and Epilim – that I was seriously ill. But the language they'd used – 'tumour likely to continue to grow', 'surgery not viable', 'right medication may stabilise the seizures' – was just vague enough to allow me to think that a cure might be possible, however unlikely. I clung to that possibility fiercely. Whenever I did try to face the idea of death, it felt dizzying, terrifying. If I managed to hold on to it for more than a few seconds at a time, it reminded me of those moments when, as a small child alone in bed, I'd contemplate the idea of death. My father had always been keen to remind us of the reality of death, while rubbishing any spiritual belief in an afterlife that might offer some crumb of comfort. And in those moments, I'd glimpsed a sliver of the stark alternative: nothingness.

So Breeda's visit was a very comforting distraction. She and I had been close friends for some years. Although we'd known each other since childhood, our friendship had blossomed again in the wake of Nic's death. She appeared one summer's day when Nicola was about nine months old and she never really left. She was a constant support, often, I'm sure, giving up her own spare time to keep me company in my long nights as a bereft lone parent. She has a special loving energy, a straightforward, calm approach to whatever is happening, and an irrepressible sense of fun. Just then, this was exactly what I needed.

'Okay, Rachel, they're going to discharge you this afternoon, so I've decided you're staying at mine! Before that we're going to go to the pub. For the next few hours, we are going to forget all about this and just have a bit of fun . . . You've probably a long road ahead of you now, I know – and by the way, I don't believe for a single moment what the doc says about just two years! So, let's have a break from it all and start as we mean to go on.'

It was the best thing anyone could have said. To shelve the seriousness, to forget about hushed voices and concerned glances, to escape the awful clinical smell of the hospital and the desperately worried faces of loved ones. Breeda helped me pack up the few belongings I had with me, came with me to sign my discharge papers and collect my medication, prescriptions and letter for the

GP, and then we just walked out of there. My beautiful Nicola was fine, staying with my mum, whom she adored. Just for the night, I was going to pretend that nothing of the past two days had happened and that I was just a regular person having a night at a close girlfriend's house.

Three

1998–2005

The years immediately after Nic's death were very, very tough. Looking back, I realise that I was very likely suffering from complex post-traumatic stress disorder, but at the time I didn't have the perspective to recognise this, and nor did those around me. Once Nicola was born – this baby that Nic and I had been so joyfully looking forward to, but to whom, now that he was gone, I had nothing left to give – I went into survival mode, merely subsisting from day to day, trying to meet the demands of a fretful newborn, too exhausted and emotionally numb to do anything more than live hour to hour or do much more than the very basics.

I was unable to sleep. In the first few years, Nicola would wake up every twenty minutes throughout the night, but also, each time I closed my eyes, I was bombarded by visceral flashbacks of Nic's death. The horror of seeing Nic die, when all I could do was stand by and watch, had left an indelible mark, caused me to shut down, to retreat from life. I had no outlet for my shock and pain or any realistic sense of the extent to which I'd been left traumatised and disempowered.

In the months and first few years that followed, I was on autopilot, unable to really reach out and ask for help; I didn't know I needed help or, in fact, that I could be helped. I was living elementally. Breathe in, breathe out, rise, feed and change Nicola, shower, eat, sleep, or at least try to. And – repeat. I insisted on staying in the house that had been my home with Nic – a lovely house but geographically quite isolated. It was an idyllic spot for a couple newly in love, but completely wrong for a young widow living on her own with her first baby to care for, and not within easy reach of people I could rely on. Although, of course, friends and family were around, I was determined to maintain my independence and give the impression that I was coping admirably. But every day was a long, lonely slog, trying to keep up with Nicola's basic care needs during the daylight hours, and waiting and longing for early evening finally to come. Then I knew I would have a few short hours of release, when I could open a bottle of wine and drink. By the time I'd finished the bottle, the tears would come, slowly at first, then in great, wrenching sobs. As at other times in my life, alcohol seemed to be the only thing that enabled me to feel something, unlocking the conflicting emotions and unexpressed hurt that I usually kept tamped down so deeply, and which worked to deaden my everyday life. For a short time each evening, drinking softened the edges of that densely impacted pain and I got some small respite. My alcohol-filled hours also allowed me to feel some connection to Nic and Dominic. As the drink took effect, the barriers I had put in place to keep my emotions in check, just so I could keep going, would slowly crumble and I was able to let the memories, the grief and the pain wash over me. I welcomed it, in some bizarre way. Much like diving, it gave me the opportunity to immerse myself in a world outside of the everyday, and while staying there would have been impossible, a visit allowed me to tap into something primal, some part of me beyond rational understanding but which I somehow knew I had to experience to stay alive.

In some ways, then, it hardly seems surprising that when the first signs began to appear that all was not well with me physically, I barely registered them. I certainly wasn't able to recognise that something serious was happening and that I needed to seek medical help. Occasionally I would lose power in my left arm. When I wanted to reach out and pick something up, I would momentarily be at a loss; I couldn't make my arm move, no matter how much I focused on trying to make it respond. Sometimes, out doing errands in the village, when I jumped back into my car to drive home I'd experience a kind of mental blank, albeit very brief. I'd find myself staring at my hand on the gearstick, unsure of what to do next. It was disconcerting, especially with something that normally came to me automatically. But I just put it down to exhaustion, lack of sleep, grief or the stress of having to care for a small child on my own – a child who reminded me of my beloved Nic every time I looked at her.

Some months later, something very frightening happened on my way back from Skibbereen, the local town. I suddenly felt compelled to stick my head out of the open driver's side window. It wasn't something I wanted to do – it's difficult and dangerous, apart from anything else – but it was as if individual parts of my body took on a will of their own. Yet while this was all very odd, somehow, I still didn't give it much thought – mostly, probably, because I was so bone-weary all the time.

When it came to the issue of my left arm not working properly, I excused it because it reminded me of times in my late teens and very early twenties when the same kind of thing had occurred and always when I felt particularly anxious, upset or under pressure. On one occasion a girlfriend had insisted that I go to the ER with her to get it checked out – this was when I was living in Dublin – and we'd gone to St Vincent's Hospital. The staff ran some routine tests and performed a lumbar puncture, and then sent me on my way. I still have a vivid memory of arriving back to our lodgings at the YWCA, feeling so ill after the procedure that I collapsed on the front steps, vomiting, my head pounding. However, when the hospital doctor got back to me with my results, he'd suggested that there was nothing wrong with me physically, and that the most likely explanation was that I was suffering from some kind of adolescent hysterical reaction; that the problem with my arm was a physical symptom of some deeper emotional problem. At the time, I'd accepted this with a familiar sense of shame. I was so uncertain of myself, so distrustful of my own perceptions and sensations, that I was all too ready to trust the instincts of others over my own. In hindsight, I find myself wondering if these were early foreshadowings of the congenital condition which was about to change my life irrevocably.

As time went on, such unusual physical occurrences became more frequent, and still I kept going. By this stage, I was becoming more and more unsettled and frightened by whatever was happening to me. Sometimes, when I tried to get out of bed during the night to go to Nicola, I'd completely lose the use of my left leg and the only way I could get to her room was by crawling on all fours.

Then there was the time I was lying in bed – trying, and failing, to fall asleep – when suddenly my left arm shot up above my head and I was unable to lower it again, no matter how much I willed it to happen. On that occasion, I decided to call a woman I was friendly with in Cork at the time, as I was really frightened and needed to talk to someone. Although she was very sympathetic, and indeed kind enough to answer my 3 a.m. call in the first place, her immediate suggestion was that I was somehow 'possessed'; that the devil had entered my body and was trying to take me over so that 'he could use me for his purposes'. It wasn't the most reassuring thing to be told in the middle of the night when I was alone except for my small daughter in a house in the middle of nowhere.

I had known that my friend was a bit of a religious fanatic, but this was too much! I thanked her for her support and got off the phone as quickly as I could. Desperate as I often felt around that time, I wasn't quite ready to accept the possibility that I might be becoming an agent of Satan.

During this period, when Nicola was about six years old, a lovely distraction came into our lives in the shape of Don, a young English diver who was in the Glandore area for the summer months. In his late twenties, outgoing and laid-back, Don had the same sunny disposition shared by many of the English divers I have met. He seemed to enjoy our company and Nicola took to him straight away, as did I. It hadn't escaped my notice either that Don was tanned and good-looking, or that there was something of a spark between us. Sure, it was light-hearted and playful rather than the deep connection I had felt with Nic, but the very fact that I noticed another man was attractive was significant; a sign, perhaps, that I was finally beginning to emerge from the darkness of my grief.

Don enjoyed the sea as much as I did, and his enthusiasm soon rekindled my own interest in diving, which had lain dormant since Nic died. After much cajoling, I eventually agreed to go diving with him and, for the first time since Nic's death, I dived to the beautiful ocean floor once again. Something began to reawaken in me – a renewed interest in life and a fleeting hint, however subdued, that life might yet hold joy and happiness for me.

A few days later I was in the kitchen making tea when once again, as I reached to lift the kettle, my left arm shot up in the air, defying all my efforts to control it. One minute I was thinking that this kind of occurrence was becoming the norm and that maybe I should visit my GP, and the next . . . a loud shriek and then nothingness.

When I came to – and to this day, I have no idea how long I lay unconscious – Nicola was sitting astride me, pulling at my arms and crying, 'Mummy, Mummy, wake up . . . Please don't die! Mummy?!'

Pushing through overwhelming fatigue, I managed to whisper to Nicola that she needed to fetch the phone from the hall. When she came back, I had to summon every ounce of mental energy to call out the digits of my mother's home number so that Nicola could key them in. I had no idea what was happening; I felt like I'd been hit by a train.

My mother realised straight away from my voice that something was badly wrong, and within fifteen minutes she arrived and, shortly afterwards, our GP, Martina, took a quick look at me, asked Nicola what had happened and then rang the local hospital, demanding that they immediately send an emergency ambulance. As we waited, she told my mother that she should take Nicola away and leave her with someone who could look after her so that my mother could join us in the hospital afterwards.

It was only a long time later that I realised that Martina, suspecting I'd had a massive seizure and anticipating that I was very likely about to have another one, had asked my mother to take Nicola so that neither of them would be there to witness another seizure event.

Inside the ambulance, a paramedic monitored me as we rushed to Cork University Hospital. Even in my confused state, I was keenly aware of a sense of urgency and of his obvious concern as I tried my best to give him some kind of account of what had happened.

In the midst of it all, the fleeting realisation came to me that if this had transpired just a few days earlier, when I was gliding along on my first diving foray in years, I would have shared the same fate as Nic and drowned in the element in which I had always felt most alive. In some ways, the thought of being there with him was not an unpleasant one. The years since he had died had been such a struggle, but now I had Nicola, and I knew her presence, her absolute need for me to be there and to be her mother, anchored me to life in the present. I could not simply drift away, no matter how much I might have longed to at the time.

Four

After I'd been diagnosed with the AVM, I was sent home with enough anti-seizure medication to open a small pharmacy, an assurance that I would adapt to the new drug regimen in time, and a huge A3 envelope containing my scans – and very little else, really. Other than the drugs, there was no agreed treatment plan, nor was there any concrete prognosis. Worst of all, I'd been offered very little by way of hope or suggested measures I could proactively take which might buy me some more time.

Simply resigning myself to my 'fate' has never been a part of my makeup. But for an initial period, before I could rally myself, I was so numbed by the cocktail of drugs and so battered by tragedy – the loss of Dominic, then Nic, my father dying just a year later, and Nicola losing her sight in one eye at just over one year old – that I simply couldn't take on board the full import of the situation. Once more, overnight, everything had changed. Things I'd regarded as certainties could no longer be taken for granted, and the most basic tenets of everyday life had been wrested from me without warning.

While I'd felt bereft and alone after Nic's death, and isolated from friends and most of my family as I adapted to being a lone parent living in a rural area, at least I'd had my independence – something which had always been incredibly important to me. After my diagnosis and discharge, however, my freedom was curtailed in many small but fundamental ways. As soon as I reported my condition to the driving authorities (which I was legally bound to do), my licence was revoked. This left me completely dependent on others for the most basic things. I could no longer do the school run for Nicola; I couldn't drive to the shops; I certainly couldn't take the car for an impromptu visit to a girlfriend's house. I had to live with the knowledge that if there was an emergency and something happened to Nicola, I'd have to wait for help to arrive rather than being able to take her myself to the out-of-hours doctor or the pharmacy. I couldn't even have a full bath any longer, in case I had a seizure and drowned, and just in case something happened, I also had to carry large batches of back-up meds wherever I went, even if only to stay overnight at my mother's. Humiliatingly, this included liquid Valium capsules and, in the event someone found me having a seizure, instructions on how they should be administered – rectally.

Whatever else could be said about my family, simply accepting the inevitable had never been their way either. During the time I was adjusting to my new drugs regimen, a family meeting was called, which included my three older brothers (two of whom were living in South Africa part-time) and Nic's family, particularly his sister, Jane, who was based in Taunton in Somerset but with whom I'd kept in touch over the years. I was at this meeting myself, of course, although now that I was on huge doses of Epilim I was given to falling asleep at any moment. The fact that everyone had come together from various far-flung locations was another clear indicator that the situation was serious, but again, this didn't really seem to sink into my awareness at the time.

The upshot of the family 'conference' was that a second – and a third and, if needs be, a fourth – medical opinion should be sought and that we'd exhaust every available avenue to see what, if any, treatment options might be viable. I remember feeling very supported and loved at this time by everyone – family and friends alike – even if I wasn't fully aware of all the individual efforts people were making. This was an era when the internet as a research tool was just coming into its own, and a lot of time was invested in finding out more about my condition and about which consultants in the field were doing the most successful, pioneering work.

One of the earliest exploratory trips we made was to the Beaumont hospital in Dublin; it seemed the obvious first port of call. I clearly remember the journey to Dublin with Breeda and Jan, my sister-in-law, on a small plane from Cork. Although I wasn't fully conscious of it myself at the time, the biggest fear as we travelled was that I would have a seizure, the likelihood of which might be greatly increased by the pressurised, high-altitude conditions of the flight. It was a very short flight, but as we approached Dublin I began to experience strange spasms in my facial muscles. I remember seeking reassurance from Jan and Breeda, and I got it, but I later learned that they were desperately trying to minimise my anxiety by underplaying what was really happening; they'd been warned that these things were possible precursors to a major seizure.

In any case, we arrived at the Beaumont without incident. We were ushered into one of the consultant's offices in the neurology department, all three of us hopeful that there might be better news for me than there had been in Cork. It was not to be. With hardly a greeting, the doctor took the envelope of scans out of my hands and slapped the first one unceremoniously on to the screen in front of him. Seconds later, after he'd taken in the sight of the large black mass around the brain on the right-hand side, he slid the scan back down and handed it to me again.

'I'm sorry, there's nothing we can do for you here, Rachel . . . nothing at all.'

Before I could gather my thoughts, Breeda and Jan began asking questions, trying to keep their voices even and measured.

'But . . . are you absolutely sure? There must be something. You're saying you can't help Rachel at all here?'

'I don't think so. This is a very complicated condition and I doubt you'll find a neurologist in this country who'll say any different. I'm so sorry.'

And that was it. No words of comfort, no gentleness, no compassion. I felt silenced, and altogether lost.

Over the next few months, Breeda and I, and sometimes Jan, undertook several trips to London to search for help – ideally, a surgeon who'd be willing to operate. We visited hospitals where, according to our research, ground-breaking work in neurosurgery was being done. Each time, it was the same routine. We'd go to see a neurology team, produce my scans and medical notes and, once these had been thoroughly perused, an expert opinion would be given. Unfortunately, each time the conclusion was the same: 'We're sorry, Rachel – there's nothing we can do for you.' At least the news was delivered in a kinder, more gentle way than at the Beaumont. However, several of the doctors went so far as to advise that I start putting my affairs in order. They were all deeply sorry and wished me well.

I don't know how I would have managed any of this without Breeda, not just because I needed someone to be with me at all times in a physical sense, especially when travelling, but also because of her ability to stay grounded and strong and her fine sense of humour. Each time we were knocked back by another hopeless prognosis from a leading neurologist, we'd head to a pub, have a gin and tonic and a cigarette, laugh and engage in whatever conversation and distraction was on offer, in the same way we'd been doing since we were in our teens. No doubt those eminent neurologists would have shuddered had they known, but it was the only way I was able to get through that time, when no hope or medical help seemed to be on the horizon.

It was around then that the reality of my situation began to sink in, finally. When 'experts' repeatedly tell you that making a will might be prudent, it gets harder and harder to sidestep the truth. I began to realise that this wasn't going to go away; I was seriously ill and, possibly, had little time left to live. The process of coming to terms with what was likely to happen was gradual, incremental. There was no 'lightbulb' moment. It happened slowly, and there was a precariousness to it that meant I could just as easily take a step back or fall down as move forward, like a toddler learning to walk. Eventually it hit me, and every cell in my body protested at the idea of leaving behind my beautiful daughter with neither a father nor a mother to look out for her. The thought filled me with dread. I knew that not knowing her father had been a heavy blow to Nicola, and I was convinced that losing her mother would be something from which she'd never recover.

By the time we returned to West Cork after our travels in London, I was struggling with a sense of complete hopelessness – and helplessness. Physically, I was a mess – weak, exhausted, and becoming increasingly dependent on other people. And now I was psychologically at rock bottom too. Part of me didn't recognise myself. I'd survived so much, yet I'd always managed to just keep going, stubbornly putting one foot in front of the other, no matter what the circumstances. But now, I felt utterly defeated.

◆ ◆ ◆

Fortunately for me, in the meantime, my family and close friends had been pressing ahead with their research into cutting-edge treatments. Every avenue was explored, although at the time I was not fully cognisant of all their efforts. People in my small seaside community were also incredibly supportive, with neighbours and acquaintances rallying around with small kindnesses, such as cards and prayers. In retrospect, I can see just how much support and encouragement I was given, and for this I will always be very grateful.

It was actually Nic's sister Jane who was instrumental in finding a way beyond the impasse. She had been making inquiries far and wide on my behalf, and it turned out that the father of one of her neighbours in Taunton was a neurologist at one of the London hospitals. It was Jane who suggested that we contact Ken Zilkha, an eminent consultant neurologist known for his ground-breaking work, then based at the Cromwell Hospital. Born in 1929, Dr Zilkha was in his late seventies but still very much a leader in his field. Another invaluable resource we discovered around this time was the Barrow Institute in Arizona, regarded as one of the world's best centres for ground-breaking neurology.

When we contacted Dr Zilkha, he agreed to look at my case and invited me to London to meet him. He insisted, however, that I should not fly and instead make the journey by ferry, to minimise the risk of further devastating seizures. When we met, Dr Zilkha suggested that we should approach Andy Molyneux, a neuro-radiologist and neuro-technician who for many years had been doing innovative work in the minimally invasive endovascular treatment of brain aneurysms and AVMs: we could contact him at the Cromwell Hospital. Andy quickly came back to us, proposing that gamma knife 'surgery' – something he was specialising in at the time – might be an option for me. Gamma knife 'surgery' is not actually surgery at all but a non-invasive procedure using radiation beams which can focus with great precision on a tumour; it is most commonly used in the brain, head and neck. Since it doesn't involve any invasive treatment in the conventional sense, damage to healthy tissue and other side effects are greatly reduced, so it is often used on patients for whom traditional methods of open surgery are not viable.

Suddenly it seemed that perhaps some form of treatment for me might ultimately be possible. At the time, the use of the gamma knife was still experimental stuff, but I wasn't going to let that deter me. Or the fact that being a very expensive procedure, we would somehow have to fund it ourselves, since there were already rumblings from my insurance company that they would not be covering any treatment which wasn't available to me in Ireland. So we asked Andy Molyneux to take a more detailed look at my case and sent him copies of my scans and notes and other medical information.

Days later he got back in touch to say that, no, the treatment wouldn't be feasible after all. The AVM, and the associated mesh of blood vessels, was much too large for it to be workable. Andy was extremely sympathetic to my predicament, however, and asked us to keep in touch in case there was anything further he could do to help. Once more, it seemed that my case was hopeless.

The next significant development came when another surgeon, Richard Nelson, contacted us as a result of Ken Zilkha's enquiries. A consultant at the Frenchay Hospital in Bristol at the time, Nelson had a formidable reputation as a pioneering neurosurgeon who was prepared to perform high-risk procedures others would shy away from. He asked us to send over my scans so that he could assess what level of risk open surgery on the AVM might involve. After this, to our amazement and delight, Nelson wrote back to say that he was prepared to 'give it a go' – if that's what I wanted. His letter made it one hundred per cent clear that the decision, and the consequences of going ahead with the surgery, would be entirely my responsibility to shoulder. In terms of what results I could expect, he stated the case in very simple terms: there was no absolute guarantee that I would survive surgery, and if I did, I would almost certainly be left with some paralysis on the left side of my body, although it was impossible to say what the degree of paralysis might be.

Looking back, I realise that this was a huge decision, one that many people would rightly find very difficult, given all the factors to be taken into consideration. Decisions of such magnitude demand serious reflection, or at least they should for most of us. But at the time, for me, it all seemed very simple. If I didn't have the surgery, I would most certainly die – within the next few years at the outside – and what I wanted most was to live and to be around for my daughter. As for the prospect of being paralysed, if it was a choice between this and dying, it wasn't something to even be taken into account; at least I would be alive and able in some shape or form to be present in Nicola's life and her future. So I wanted the surgery, no matter what. My decision was already made, and I saw no point in wasting any more time.

I can see now that I was operating on a very elemental level and I was largely incapable of teasing out any real thoughts or feelings about the situation. The doses of the various anti-seizure drugs I was taking had been incrementally increased over the months since my diagnosis, so it's no exaggeration to say I was living a kind of emotional half-life, with my awareness and mental processes blunted. In any case, the urge to survive and the primal need to look after my daughter at all costs were strong enough to trump everything else.

I told Richard Nelson that I wanted to proceed with the surgery. He agreed, although at no point did he ask to meet me. This is fairly unusual in the medical world and meant that I wouldn't set eyes on the man who was offering to try to save my life until the day before he operated on me. Nelson and his team were keen that the surgery be scheduled as quickly as possible; this was late 2005. Because Christmas was fast approaching, however, I absolutely insisted that I needed to spend the festive season with Nicola in case it might be our last one together. This was agreed to, albeit slightly reluctantly, and the date for the surgery – which would take place at the Frenchay Hospital in Bristol under the auspices of Ken Zilkha as my primary consultant – was fixed for early in the New Year: 6 January 2006.

However, before the main surgery, and before Christmas, I would have to have a preparatory procedure at the Cromwell. As Richard Nelson explained, one of his biggest concerns about performing the operation was the possibility that I would bleed to death on the operating table as he was excising the AVM, mainly because it was so large and had so many feeding and draining arteries and veins within it. To address this, he needed somehow to find a way of stopping, or at least vastly reducing, the circulation of blood within the AVM before the main surgery took place.

At this point, Andy Molyneux once more became involved. One of his main areas of innovation over several decades was the minimally invasive treatment of AVMs and brain aneurysms via the vascular system, and he was able to propose a cutting-edge solution for my problem. This would involve the insertion of a tiny quantity of surgical 'glue' into a main artery of the AVM, which would solidify quickly and effectively reduce some of the volume of blood from filling the tumour. Embolisation, they call it. This was a non-invasive procedure, carried out via a catheter inserted into the groin and fed up towards the brain, and would require a great degree of precision and skill on the part of the surgeon. Andy explained that the glue would have to be deposited at the exact moment of the peak of the heartbeat, at the fullest dilation of the artery, so that when the heart came off the beat, the glue would lodge in the artery. The precision of the timing, and the exact volume of glue to be used, was absolutely critical. Too little glue, and it would escape into the pulmonary system and cause a potentially fatal stroke; placed too early or too late, the same outcome.

Within a few short weeks, the date for this procedure had come around. I don't remember much of the period leading up to it, but others have told me that I seemed pretty unfazed, despite the fact that the procedure was still experimental, would involve a precarious and exacting process for the surgeons, and, as Andy Molyneux warned me, I would have to be partially conscious throughout, to enable my responses and vital signs to be carefully monitored. Again, my guess is that any anxieties were overridden by the inescapable awareness that the alternative was that I would die within a short space of time. And I can't reiterate enough the extent to which I was functioning without my usual clarity and ability to anticipate what lay ahead. I also knew that, compared to what I would have to undergo in the New Year – Richard Nelson had estimated that the surgery could last up to twelve hours – this pre-op procedure was relatively 'small potatoes'.

Meanwhile, a minor battle of sorts had been ongoing between my health insurance company and my solicitor, Richard Martin. When I mentioned in a casual conversation with Richard that the insurance company was refusing to cover or reimburse any of my medical costs at the Cromwell, he was outraged and vowed to help me. He was successful in pursuing a case against them and obtained a commitment from them to at least partially pay for my expenses – the preparatory procedure, if not the accommodation costs – and he refused to accept any fee at all for doing so.

Yet again, I don't know what I would have done without family and friends. Throughout this entire period, my brothers and their wives cared for Nicola and took it in turns to be my support

41

and companions. Once more they accompanied me on the onward journey to the Cromwell Hospital. When I arrived, I realised I hadn't even brought a change of clothes, let alone an overnight bag, and Jan was kind enough to go out shopping while I was going through the pre-op tests. In my state of mind, I hadn't even anticipated that I'd need pyjamas, a bathrobe and some basic cosmetics for what might be a stay of up to a week at the Cromwell. I guess I was just very ill, exhausted and bewildered.

◆ ◆ ◆

As I began to come around in the recovery suite, I became aware of a young nurse standing over me, holding one of my hands and softly saying my name. I hadn't been fully unconscious during the procedure but had been given enough sedatives to produce a kind of 'twilight' effect, which meant that now I couldn't recall anything of the time I'd been in the operating room. In my groggy and confused state, I remember thinking that I was still here, still alive, and that it must have gone okay, and trying to smile weakly up at the young nurse.

And suddenly I was screaming. A loud, high-pitched shriek over which I had no control was pushing its way out of me and all I could do was submit to a sense of absolute terror. The last thing I remember was the nurse rushing to press the call button above my bed and shouting for immediate assistance: 'Guys, guys, she's seizing—'

And then, nothing.

When I woke up, I was in a different place – the ICU, as I would later learn. I felt incredibly weak and had an unbearable, searing pain on one side of my head. This time, it was not a nurse standing beside me but Dr Zilkha, looking down at me with eyes full of concern and kindness. Seeing that I was beginning to stir, he set his hand on the top of my head and said gently, 'You poor thing . . . You poor thing.'

That simple gesture, and those words from this kindly elderly man, completely broke me. I sobbed and sobbed. I was crying for myself, for the pain and the uncertainty and the fear of dying which had been part of my world now for so many weeks and months. I was crying again for Nic, my soulmate and husband, and for Dominic, the brother who had been like the other half of me. I was crying for Nicola and the fierce love I had for her which meant that I couldn't just let go of life and of all this pain. And Dr Zilkha stood there as I cried, his hand resting on my head, eyes full of compassion for my suffering.

Then, once again, I heard the screaming I didn't recognise as mine and I blacked out. Another massive seizure plunged me into oblivion once more.

I ended up having to stay in the Cromwell hospital for a full week. The 'glue' procedure had gone well, but repeated seizures in the aftermath left me wiped out. Every so often I would be seized by an outburst of emotion which seemed to come out of nowhere and over which I had absolutely no control. The rest of the time, everything just felt grey and colourless. Before finally being moved to a recovery room, I spent a few more days in the high-dependency unit while my medication was being adjusted and gradually increased, in an attempt to restore some stability to my brain and prevent further seizures. Then I simply headed home, back to West Cork, to await surgery.

Five

I fell in love with Nic Gotto's voice before I set eyes on him. It was the summer of 1994, and I'd recently returned to Glandore from the UK, where I'd spent a few years working in the hospitality industry, to open my own bistro in the converted premises of The Pier House, our old family home. I'd heard his name mentioned before by my brother, in their conversations about the family chandlery business; as a fisherman and a diver, Nic was someone they'd had dealings with now and again. The first time I heard his voice was when I was working behind the bar area in the bistro, for which I'd kept the original name, The Pier House. As I knelt down below the countertop to rearrange some bottles, I was struck by the deep, resonant tones of a newly arrived customer who was clearly joining a group on the far side of the room. I could tell that his friends were pleased to see him, and that the feeling was mutual, as he greeted them in a rich, well-spoken English accent. Although the voice was 'sophisticated', its owner spoke with a lively, relaxed good humour and without a trace of pretentiousness. I was intrigued enough to straighten up and have a quick look, but he was around the corner so I couldn't quite glimpse the new arrival. I got back to work and didn't think any more about it.

A couple of days later, around the same time – early afternoon – I heard the voice again and, as before, I felt immediately drawn to its owner. This time, though, I made sure to have a proper look, and was able to determine that the lovely voice belonged to a very tall, athletic seafaring type with a close-cropped blond, balding head, sea- and wind-tanned skin, blue-green eyes and a smile that instantly lit up the room. I reckoned he was perhaps in his mid- to late thirties – a man who seemed comfortable in his own skin and had a quiet, self-contained air of confidence about him which was very attractive to me.

We have form for this in my family – falling in love with our future husband's voice before we even see them, that is. The same thing happened when my mother first encountered my father, back in the mid-1950s in the north of England. She was nineteen years old to his forty-two, working as an illustrator at a grass research station near Harrogate; he was involved in a project to regenerate the sports fields of schools in the area, which had been used in the land effort during the war. In the office where Mum worked, her desk was stationed behind a partition, and so the first few times my father called in to discuss an aspect of the project with one of the managers, she'd heard his sonorous, melodic voice from behind her partition without ever actually catching a glimpse of him. Perhaps it was his thespian background (his parents had been actors in a travelling Shakespearian theatre company), but whatever the explanation, my father had a very self-assured manner of speaking and could easily command the attention of a room with his incisive pronunciation and clear delivery. Although a very handsome man, physically he was short and slight of stature, so it's possible that he used the asset of his voice to bolster his presence. Once they actually met face to face, my mother quickly fell in love with this much older man, while he was clearly charmed by her, an artistically gifted, self-effacing and beautiful young woman. Before long, she had accepted his proposal of marriage.

Things didn't move quite as swiftly between Nic and me, but as far as whirlwind romances go, we weren't too far behind. One very pragmatic reason why we didn't get together immediately was the fact that, at the time, I was having a flirtation with a married man named Jonathan – a charismatic and much older guy who had pursued me relentlessly for several months before I'd finally agreed to go out to dinner with him. An occasional visitor to the village, he was charming, cultured and highly intelligent. He was also smitten with me, and I greatly enjoyed his company – and, admittedly, the attention he lavished on me. However, when I met Nic, I knew immediately that it was different, sensing straight away that he was going to be a very important person in my life.

Nic was also some years older than me – fourteen, to be precise; I was twenty-four to his thirty-eight. I'd always been attracted to older men, while they seemed very much drawn to me. Before Nic, each time I'd got involved in one of these relationships it had nearly always ended badly, particularly for me, as I discovered that the apparent thrill of being with someone unattainable and emotionally unavailable, and who would inevitably tire of me, was ultimately only damaging and left me feeling worthless. During my time in Dublin, after I'd left home in Glandore at seventeen and ended up living in the city, I'd had a few relationships with older men and learned the hard way that there was a very fine line between being flattered and spoiled, wined and dined and then feeling empty and lost when there was no substance to the relationship. I was looking for love and they were looking for sex. These short-lived romances would invariably end in tears as I was too needy to allow a relationship to find its natural legs. I needed commitment, and as soon as I began the search for confirmation that this was it, that we were to spend the rest of our days together, they'd move on as resolutely as they'd pursued me in the first place. Looking back, I can see I was longing for some form of connection and would have taken the first man who looked at me.

But intuitively I knew in my heart that Nic was different – and, for once, in a very good way. He was the first man who ever loved me for me, for the person that I was, rather than as a trophy younger woman who'd flatter his ego and look good on his arm. Put simply, he utterly adored me, right from the very start.

However, Nic was so relaxed and chivalrous that initially I didn't realise how interested he was in me. I knew I was greatly drawn to him, but I was very much caught up with my other flirtation and wasn't at all sure what this tall, 'upmarket hippy' type made of me. But my brother Dominic's girlfriend, Lauraine, who worked alongside me in the bar and bistro that summer, had noticed that his passing visits to have a quick coffee and chat with us at less busy times had become more frequent.

'That guy Nic Gotto's very nice, isn't he?' Lauraine remarked one day at work, with a wickedly teasing look. Unexpectedly, I felt myself redden a little as she deliberately poked her face in mine with a knowing grin. Laughing a little, I smirked back at her because the truth was that I was secretly becoming very attracted to Nic Gotto. I didn't, however, harbour much hope that he might have any real interest in me because I was, after all, obviously so many years his junior, and he seemed so worldly and grown up in comparison to my young twenty-four years. Inwardly, I was delighted at Lauraine's searching remark, but rather than give her any satisfaction I deliber-ately feigned a look of mock indifference and busily carried on with what I was doing. I'd felt my pulse jump a little, though, and idly wondered if Nic's frequent visits were simply platonic or whether they had another, more meaningful reason.

At that moment, a group of tourists came in, so I didn't have time to think any more about it for a while. Besides, I was due to meet Jonathan later; it was one of my rare nights off, and we had agreed to meet along the coast for dinner. I felt a flutter of antic- ipation; our evenings together were always fun and light-hearted and I loved the conversation.

I was feeling good about myself, it was a beautiful summer evening, and a handsome man would be meeting me for an evening of good wine and fun. During the few years that had passed since I'd returned to Glandore, to refurbish The Pier House and open the bistro, a lot of things had somehow fallen into place, and I was certainly feeling much happier and more confident than I'd ever been during my time in Dublin and, after that, Wiltshire.

And when Dominic had come back to Glandore that February, to coincide with my preparations for the opening of the restaurant that summer, bringing Lauraine with him, it seemed that things were looking up more than ever. Lauraine and I became close straight away – she was to become my lifelong best friend – and she jumped at the chance to help me with running the business. Dominic was intending to help out my brother Nicky in the family chandlery business, now that he was in the area again. Lauraine and I loved working together, and her sense of fun and her willingness to put in more than her share of hard graft chimed with my own philosophy at the time – which was to work hard and play hard.

It was on my next night off from the bistro – a few weeks after the dinner with Jonathan – that things began to take off with Nic. I was having a drink in the village, enjoying a chat with some of the regulars in the pub. All at once, my friend, the owner, appeared behind the bar, shouting that there was a call for me in the hall (this was in the days before mobiles). He beckoned at me to come over: apparently, Lauraine was calling from The Pier House. 'It sounds quite urgent, Rachel,' he said as I took the receiver.

'Hi, Lauraine – everything okay?' I'm sure my voice held more than a note of concern – I knew that Lauraine would contact me on my night off only if it was urgent, as she was more than capable of running the show.

'Rachel!' – Lauraine's voice was breathless yet insistent – 'It's Nic Gotto! He's just called in here asking for you, and when I told him it was your night off he wanted to know where you'd be! He's on his way up there to you as we speak. Just thought I'd better give you a heads-up.'

'Nic Gotto? Right . . .' I felt my heart lurch and my face flushed. I couldn't deny that I was excited at the idea that Nic had come to The Pier House to seek me out, and at the prospect that I'd see him here very shortly. 'Okay – thanks, Lauraine. Jonathan said he might call in here later, but I guess I can see Nic too.' I laughed.

'Well, you'd better decide what you're going to do, and quick. I'd better go, but let me know what happens!'

The call left me flustered and buzzing with nervous excitement – a sure sign, if I needed one, that Nic was very much on my radar. For a few minutes I weighed up the possibilities, then I swiftly decided that I'd play it a little cool but still make sure that I'd get to see him. I gathered up my things and said goodbye to everyone, making as if to leave the pub. As soon as I was outside the front door, however, I bumped into Nic. As fit and athletic as he was, he was out of breath; he had clearly been in a hurry to get here.

'Rachel! So glad I caught you . . . Are you leaving? Do you have to be somewhere?'

'Nic!' I feigned my apparent surprise quite well. 'Well, yes, I was just heading back down the road, actually – it's been a long day.'

'I was hoping you'd perhaps . . . come and have a glass of wine with me. Would you like to do that?'

The gentlemanly, courteous way he spoke was more than enough to tip the balance in his favour, if indeed I'd been in any doubt that I'd love to take him up on his suggestion.

'Yes, why not? I would like that – I'll have a Martini, though!'

We went back into the bar and Nic found us a table with a lovely view, set a bit apart from the regular crowd. For the next couple of hours, we enjoyed an easy, relaxed conversation, where the special energy between us seemed to open up and flow. It felt as if we had a lot in common, including, perhaps most importantly, our love of the sea.

Nic was Anglo-Irish. His family was English and had come to Carrigaline in Cork sometime in the 1950s. In the earlier part of his life he had followed the traditional path set down by previous generations of Gotto men: prep school, then school at Harrow in England. After that, he'd gone to Trinity College Dublin, where he studied Psychology because the college wasn't running the Marine Biology programme that year. As soon as this phase of his life was complete, however, and, as he saw it, he'd fulfilled his family obligations, he'd put the expectations of his family aside to follow his real passion – the sea – and had become a fisherman, shellfish farmer and scuba diver. Nic had little interest in his English middle-class background, or in the career paths his peers were expected to follow – business, banking, politics or the law. Although he could have easily pursued the same path, he loved the simple life of the sea – being around boats, fishing and, most of all, deep-sea diving. When he was in his mid-twenties, he had met a South African woman, Maggie Glicksten, with whom he had two beautiful daughters, Emily and Hayley, but by the time we met their relationship was all but over, although he still got to see his daughters regularly and absolutely adored them.

He had been working in the Glandore area for the past few months, on a joint contract with University College Cork, conducting marine research in the area. He told me he felt a great affinity with the area, and was thinking that, after his contract was over, he might look at deepening his connections to Glandore and starting up a diving business in the locality. Nic was clearly driven in his chosen field, but very much by his passion for his work rather than the prospect of 'getting ahead' purely for its own sake. Like me, he was conscious he was something of a blow-in in West Cork, and indeed in Ireland generally, but, also like me, he felt a sense of belonging and loved the people and the wild coastal landscapes.

The time talking to Nic flew by (helped by another few Martinis), and I was shocked to realise that it was already nearly midnight. It all felt so natural and easy, and the persistent undercurrent of a strong physical attraction between us was undeniable. Eventually, when I announced that I was tired and needed to go home – I had an early start the next morning – Nic was attentive and considerate and courteously offered to walk me home. With any other man, I would have sensed the expectation to be invited in for coffee once there, but not with Nic.

Just as we were readying ourselves to leave the pub, however, Jonathan walked in. Feeling suddenly confused, I told Nic that I had to say a quick hello to a friend and asked him to wait where he was until I came back. I scurried over to Jonathan and tried to take him aside a little, out of Nic's view, as he eagerly stepped forward to greet me.

'Ah, Jonathan – great to see you, how was your night? Listen, I'm just about to leave here with some friends now – I'll see you tomorrow . . .'

I couldn't fail to notice the disappointment that passed over his face momentarily before he composed himself.

'Sure, sure, no problem at all . . . You go ahead with your friends, of course! But—' He craned his neck a little, trying to get a look at whoever was in the corner waiting for me. 'Why don't I come by later on? They'll be closing up here soon, so I'll just have a last drink and can call in to you on my way back to the boat.'

'Yeah, okay . . . Sure! Yes, that's fine – see you later, then.' I knew I didn't sound as enthusiastic as I would normally, but I was keen to get away, and back to Nic, as soon as possible. By now I was unable to think straight about what now seemed like a complicated situation. Nothing had happened between Nic and me, but already I knew I felt a connection which couldn't be ignored.

When I got back to the table, Nic was as gentlemanly and composed as ever. If he had seen anything of the exchange or the telling body language between me and Jonathan, he certainly wasn't intrusive enough to ask any questions.

Once we arrived at my front door, Nic leaned down to kiss me on the cheek and asked if he could have breakfast with me the following morning. Delighted, I immediately agreed to meet him at the bistro before my working day began. As I shut the door, I felt wonderfully calm, yet deeply excited too. I was blown away by his considerate gallantry and feeling more and more intrigued.

An hour or so later, when I was climbing into my bed, there was a knock at the door. As I got up to see who was there, I remember thinking that it might be Nic – perhaps he wasn't going to turn out to be so gallant after all! But it wasn't him; it was Jonathan, of course. I let him in and together we wound our way up the stairs. He was a romantic man and was passionate about me, and I guess in that moment I was happy about that.

But on that particular night, after the lovely, special time I'd just spent with Nic, for the first time, Jonathan's amorous overtures didn't leave me feeling quite as special. My mind still held on to the lovely atmosphere I'd felt with Nic earlier. Things with Jonathan suddenly seemed slightly empty.

Not long after that, I told Jonathan that I'd met someone. I thought he'd accept it easily, but he was desperately upset. He'd been talking about telling his wife about us for some time, but girlfriends I'd confided in had told me this was unlikely ever to happen; that it was just what men said in these situations, to keep the affair alive and maybe to ease their own conscience a little.

Anyway, I wasn't entirely sure I wanted him to break up his family for me. I was in my early twenties and was having fun with my life, and I didn't know if I could envisage a long-term future with this man, as charismatic and interesting as he seemed.

So when I told him we weren't going to meet any more, I was slightly shocked by his reaction. He seemed distraught. But while he didn't want to lose me, at the same time, he did let me go with a smile. Deep down, perhaps, he knew he was unlikely to enter into a long-term relationship with me, and besides, he had many commitments and lived far away.

Now that the way was clear for me and Nic, things happened very quickly. In fact, it was fortunate that I ended the relationship with Jonathan when I did, for just a matter of days after I last saw Nic he got in touch again and asked if I wanted to meet him for lunch the next day. He'd be coming into Glandore Harbour by boat – he was in the area again for work – and said he was very keen to see me again. By this time, we'd only met up a couple of times, and it had been less than a few months since we'd had that first drink. I said that of course I'd be delighted to see him.

So he came to my flat above the bistro for coffee. Almost as soon as he arrived he told me that he had something important to say to me.

'Rachel, I already know that I want to make a life with you . . . Why don't we move in together, straight away?'

I was flabbergasted yet excited. I hadn't been expecting to be considering something like this quite so early on, but my first response was shocked delight. As I've said, I knew from the moment I first met Nic that he was somehow going to be very important in my life.

As I gathered my thoughts, Nic continued: 'I'm due to go back to Oysterhaven later tonight anyway . . . So why don't I just pack my stuff when I get there and come to live with you for the time being, until we can get something more permanent sorted out?'

Again, I was astonished, flattered and, strangely, very happy – full of joy that he was so clear and decisive about what he wanted. So I nodded and agreed to his plan, assuring him that I couldn't be happier. When he left some hours later, after a sweet afternoon together, the first thing I did was to get on the phone to Lauraine and Jan.

'Hey! You'll never guess what . . . Nic's just been here and said he wants us to live together. In fact, he's gone to his house to pack all his stuff right now and says he'll be back tomorrow to move in with me! Oh my God – how ridiculously fast is this all happening?! What am I going to do?'

'What, I don't believe it, Rach! And yet I do, he's a strange guy. I knew he was besotted with you, right from the start. Anyway, what do you mean, you don't know what you're going to do? You're going to live with Nic Gotto, and you'll both work it out as you go along – that's what's going to happen!'

I was hugely excited, but under the surface was a level of calm I'd never felt before in my dealings with a man. My instincts were telling me that this was a really good development and that, even though things were moving so fast, there was something profoundly right about it all. Deep down, I felt safe with this man and knew that he would bring me only good things. I felt that at last I'd met someone significant and it was going to change my life.

Six

On the twelfth day of Christmas, I took a flight from Cork to Bristol, entirely alone. My mother had driven me to Cork airport, and Jane Gotto, my sister-in-law, would be meeting me on the other side. I was travelling to undergo life-threatening brain surgery with a surgeon I'd never met, and there was no guarantee that I'd see Ireland, or my home in West Cork, ever again, but I'd insisted on boarding the plane and making the journey on my own.

Only much later did I come to understand why I was behaving in this insistently solitary way. Many people around me would have been more than happy to take that flight with me (and indeed a number of them offered to do so). Why on earth wouldn't I have welcomed the moral support and physical reassurance of a friend or family member? Deep down, it felt somehow shameful that my body had betrayed me in such a way, and I guess hidden parts of me didn't in any way feel lovable. Rather like a piece of software might corrupt a hard drive, I was responding to the 'program' installed in my earliest life; I just didn't feel worthy, and the less upset and disruption I caused to others, the better. This was the only way I knew, and besides, it left me with fewer feelings of shame and doubt. I didn't want to impose my difficulties on other people, even those closest to me. Being independent – always at one remove from loved ones and able to manage my emotions and needs without any reliance on others – had been a signature for me during the lonely years after Nic's death, when every day was no more than getting by. And since the symptoms of the growth in my brain, the AVM, and the necessary medications had begun to manifest themselves, I had become even more out of touch with my own feelings.

On that plane, staring down at the detailed patchwork of fields as we started our ascent, I thought about the Christmas just past. It hadn't really been what I'd hoped for. True, I'd spent the holidays with Nicola, but it was also a time when everyone in my immediate family felt they should be there too. My three older brothers and their wives had joined us at my mum's house for the period between Christmas Day and New Year's Eve, instead of going to their respective holiday homes in South Africa as normal. A procession of other family members and close friends had dropped in over those days as well, obviously also out of a need to see me before the surgery in January.

While I'd greatly appreciated everyone's intentions, all of this made for a rather strained, falsely jolly atmosphere, with me being very much at the centre of everything. As with many families, when adult children come together at their childhood home with their own families in tow and out of their usual routine, things were a little tense at times. I was very grateful for all their efforts, but all I'd really wanted was to spend a very peaceful, relaxing time with my daughter. So I found myself wishing more than once that I'd just taken Nicola off somewhere quiet. Yet this would have been impossible in any case, since it wasn't really that safe for me to spend time alone with my child at this point.

The truth was that I was a very different person from the person I'd been before my diagnosis, and especially since the procedure in the Cromwell. It was very hard to explain this to others. I'm not sure I even had enough awareness of myself to be able to do so, let alone the mental energy to pin down precisely how I'd changed. I knew that when people looked at me they saw more or less the same Rachel they'd always known. I'm sure that there was also an element of wanting to normalise what was happening to me, so people made a concerted effort to be the same with me as they always had been.

It was exhausting, however, and actually impossible for me to pretend that nothing had changed. I felt hollowed out, as if my brain had been fried by the seizures and nothing remained but blackened, smouldering ashes where once my clarity, drive and energy had been. I just didn't feel like Rachel any more. I was someone else now – someone whose brain had been invaded by a foreign mass; whose healthy neural tissue had so recently been tinkered with by surgeons treading experimental ground; whose electrical impulses were liable to short-circuit at any moment. Even now, it's impossible to express this sense of having been changed, of being somehow 'other'. And yet it was something I was acutely conscious of. So I just had to live with the vague awareness of not being 'me' any more. It's now common knowledge, even among those who aren't medical specialists, that people who have suffered brain injuries (or brain 'insults', as they are medically known) can experience fundamental personality changes which those around them can find very difficult to adjust to.

I couldn't manage alone, and someone suggested that I ask my friend Josephine, who lived in Canada, to come and stay until it was time for me to travel to Bristol for my surgery, and also to live with me for a little while afterwards, to help me through the initial recovery period. Josephine had kindly agreed. We'd met a few years earlier on a psychotherapy training course and had hit it off straight away, despite the fact that she was some years older than me.

Yet almost as soon as Josephine arrived, as she was unpacking her suitcases in one of the spare rooms, it became obvious that inviting her to stay had been a huge mistake. It wasn't Josephine's fault, but the problem was that she too assumed I'd be the same person, with the same levels of energy and need to connect and socialise, as when we'd first met. Because I simply wasn't that Rachel any longer, I found any expectations of me very difficult to deal with. Basically, she needed something from me – our old companionship and connection – and I just wasn't able to provide that in the same way as before. I was exhausted, physically, mentally and emotionally, and simply didn't have the wherewithal to engage with a house guest 24/7. I found the company and demands of other people generally very wearing and needed to spend the majority of time on my own. It was the only way I could ensure that I would be able to tolerate the company of others for very limited periods.

Eventually, Josephine decided of her own accord to leave, and I wasn't sorry. She missed her family and her dog too much and needed to go back to Canada. We parted strangely, without talking about things, and although I felt guilty, at the same time I was hugely relieved. Her leaving was the only way I could cope. I didn't even have the capacity to properly explain what the problem was. Previously I'd been lively and sociable, but now I felt blunted and bone-weary, as if everything was in drab monotone. These were very different times.

◆　◆　◆

So when 4 January finally came around, I was relieved that the wait for surgery was over. Jane Gotto was waiting for me at Bristol airport, and I was very glad to see her. On our way to her house, where I'd be staying the night before going to the Frenchay Hospital the next afternoon, I asked that we stop at an IKEA outlet I'd spotted. Jane accompanied me inside and was kind enough to wait when I decided I needed to buy a sofa and chair and have them shipped back to my house in Ireland. I realise this was my way of making a positive statement about my operation and my chances of survival. Either that, or I was completely in denial.

And I had my cowboy boots. My form since I'd left home and had my own money was that any time something was going wrong or I was upset I immediately went out and bought a new pair of shoes, so by this time I'd amassed a rather large collection. Purchased on one of the scouting trips to a hospital in London, my fine black leather Italian cowboy boots from Russell & Bromley would for me become the archetype and symbol of freedom. I absolutely loved them and the reassuring, solid clumping sound they made as I walked London's pavements.

The next day, Jane and I made our way to the hospital. My mum and my brother Adrian would be flying in the next morning so they could be waiting for me when I came out of theatre the following evening. The Frenchay had, and has, a reputation as an international centre of excellence for cutting-edge surgery, so I was a little surprised to discover that the neurology ward was housed in a wing of the military hospital which had previously occupied the grounds there. While of course everything had been refurbished and modernised, the original shell and structure had been kept intact, and so the neurology wards and theatres were in a low-ceilinged, narrow building typical of an old barracks.

Once I'd been admitted and Jane had left, I changed and sat on my bed, waiting for the usual obs and other pre-surgery procedures to be carried out. This was the first time that I was to meet face to face with Richard Nelson, the neurosurgeon who would lead the surgical team the following day in the very difficult and risky procedure to hopefully rid me of the lesion that was threatening to prematurely end my life. All prior communications I'd had with the man had either been by letter or through Ken Zilkha, and so I felt especially nervous in that moment as I watched him approach the bed with a colleague. Out of the two men, I was able to guess immediately which was Mr Nelson. Tall and slightly balding, this man brought with him an air of unmistakable seriousness. In greeting, he offered only a flicker of a smile, and as he shook my hand and introduced himself he addressed me as Mrs Gotto, a formality that he would maintain throughout all our future contact. The conversation was delivered in a slow and deliberate manner, as he explained how they planned to carry out the procedure the next day. Mr Nelson went into meticulous detail about the surgery, and both he and his colleague couldn't have been more respectful and informative as they carefully explained their plan. In truth, I didn't take in much of what they said at that point. I'd come to that place where I didn't want too much more information in my head. Frankly, it all horrified me, and I just wanted to get the next day over and done, for better or for worse. I'd had plenty of time in the preceding weeks to imagine the worst, I'd been through my own personal imagined horrors of what could go wrong and, at that moment, I was ready to hand myself over to this man and his team. I knew all too well that my fate was quite literally in their hands and I just had to trust that they knew what they were doing. Eventually Mr Nelson seemed satisfied that everything that needed to be said had been said and the last thing he required at that stage was for me to sign and date the consent forms for surgery. Handing back the completed forms, I heard myself let out a sigh, of what could only have been resignation, and when both doctors left my bedside I was more than content to distract myself from thinking any further about what might happen the next day by busying myself with watching the goings-on in the ward.

Just then, another patient was wheeled in on a trolley to a bed across from mine. A woman of about my age, she had lines attaching her to drips and monitors in all directions. As the trolley approached my bed, I also registered with alarm that her head was shaven on one side and she was moaning loudly and very agitated. When she saw me, she suddenly lurched forwards, ripping out some of her lines in the process. Glaring at me intensely, with vacant yet crazed eyes, she began to lunge towards me, hissing, 'I'm going to kill you . . . I'll fucking kill you!'

One of the nurses rushed forward to calm her and eased her back down on to the trolley, until she was once more lying down. Once the same nurse and her colleagues had stationed the trolley in the bay, transferred the patient on to her bed and made sure that she was a little more settled, a nurse came over to me.

'Don't worry about her, Rachel, honestly. Pippa has just come up from recovery . . . She's a bit agitated after the anaesthetic but she'll calm down very shortly. She won't remember any of this later, when she comes around properly. So don't worry – she's harmless, I can assure you.'

While these words went some way to explaining the distress my fellow patient was in, I didn't feel particularly reassured. For the next few hours, Pippa continued to writhe and moan, twisting and turning in her bed every so often. At one point, she even managed to sit up again, and once more began tearing at her lines, a look of pure hatred contorting her features, growling, 'I'm going to . . . kill—!'

A nurse hurriedly appeared and tried to quieten her down again. When she had, I called the nurse over, told her I was feeling a bit freaked out and was worried about not sleeping and asked her for something to help me sleep.

She left for a few minutes and when she returned she had a small plastic beaker of water in one hand. As she got closer, I saw a little pill in a plastic cup in the other hand.

'Here you go, dear – this should help you get some rest.'

She was right. Not long after I'd downed the pill, my eyes began to feel heavy and a pleasant, irresistible sensation of warmth and physical tiredness came over my body. Soon I was fast asleep, oblivious to Pippa in the bed opposite.

◆ ◆ ◆

The next morning, I was woken very early and made ready for theatre. I could see that Pippa was now sleeping peacefully. Well, at least that was something. In spite of the protests of the nurses, who had brought a wheelchair to take me to the operating room, I insisted that I'd be okay to walk there myself. And that's what I did. As I walked up and through the ward with a theatre nurse at my side, past Pippa and other obviously very ill patients, I felt a cold wave of fear break over me. But I kept walking. Perhaps this was the last time I'd ever be able to walk again unassisted, and I was determined to do it my way.

As I was ushered into the pre-room just outside the operating theatre, I came face to face with the man I was now entrusting with my life and my future, if I was to have any. It still felt odd that this was only the second time I had met Richard Nelson. I shook his hand and nodded around at the rest of the team; there were a lot of people who'd be assisting with my operation.

'Well, I hope you've got enough gas in those tanks, I don't want to be aware of you working inside my brain,' I quipped to the anaesthetist. Once more, I was being the old Rachel. No one else was fooled, though, and neither was I, really. This was a terrifying moment, and there was absolutely nothing I could do but hope. What happened next – my life, the quality of that life, or indeed my death – was now entirely beyond my control. I lay down and the anaesthetist asked me to count backwards. 'Ten, nine, eight—' Soon, I was out.

Seven

My first year with Nic was mostly filled with happiness, as we set about making a life together like any couple newly in love. After an initial few months living in my little two-bedroomed flat above The Pier House, he suggested that we needed something bigger, so he rented a beautiful house at the top of the village, which we moved into together. We loved each other's company and were sweet together in our new world.

I soon realised to my delight that Nic really was the lovely man I'd imagined him to be from the start – kind, very bright, wise, driven in his work but relaxed and good-humoured, and always patient and infinitely tender with me. There was no game playing, no emotional manipulation or other hidden agendas; Nic was always clear about how much he loved me and the fact that he was always there for me. He was a constant man, someone who would always be in my corner. Throughout my childhood, with my father and later with the men I'd become romantically entangled with, I'd always felt a sense of not being good enough. Men remained emotionally unavailable to me; I was never quite sure if, or how much, they really loved me and was always plagued by insecurity and doubt. Being with Nic was the first time in my life I'd ever felt truly loved and cherished and I began to grow in worth and self-esteem. I felt a bit like a new leaf unfolding in the sunlight.

During our first autumn together, Nic taught me to scuba dive, so that in time I'd be able to go diving with him and his friends. At this stage, he was involved in two research projects for UCC (University College Cork): one exploring the possibilities for sustainable scallop fishing through the use of hatching broods in semi-closed ponds, and the second involving the investigative fishing trials off the north-west coast of Ireland to check the viability of bluefin tuna fishing. Since moving to Glandore to be with me, Nic had taken the decision to also go about formalising a diving expeditions business which he'd been effectively running on a casual basis for the previous few years. That autumn, he founded Sundancer Diving Expeditions, which ran organised recreational trips for groups of divers wanting to visit some of the amazing abundance of shipwrecks off the coast of County Cork. A number of these – *U260*, the *Silver Dollar* wreck, the *Aud* and the *Kowloon Bridge* – lay at between 30 and 40 metres and were very much accessible on air. Through Sundancer, Nic also coordinated groups of more technical divers, the 'Trimix divers', who explored the wreck of the famous Cunard ocean liner the *Lusitania*, which was torpedoed off the Irish coast by a German U-Boat in May 1915 during World War 1, resulting in huge loss of life.

I was as keen to learn how to dive as Nic was to teach me. All of this was new and exciting territory for me, but I was familiar with and loved the sea so it seemed a natural evolution. I was a confident swimmer, having been around the ocean since childhood. But before meeting Nic, I had only ever snorkelled, so I felt a little hesitant at the idea of full immersion in the ocean depths, given that I'd always been prone to claustrophobia. Nic had every confidence that I would learn quickly, however, and that confidence transferred itself to me.

Not that I had much time to overthink the matter. Under Nic's tutelage, my induction to diving was a very rapid one, and shortly afterwards consisted of jumping out of a small rubber dinghy holding his hand and continuing to cling on as we swam straight away to a depth of about 20 metres. Nic had given me a few tips about how to get used to breathing from a regulator, how to clear my ears and what to do if I got in trouble, but he firmly believed that the best way for me to learn was by experience – by (literally!) being thrown in at the deep end and seeing how I got on. He was pretty gung-ho about it all, but it was the best way to help me believe in my own abilities.

After a few more short expeditions like this, always accompanied by Nic, he felt I was ready for my first dive without him. And so I jumped from the side of a boat with a marine biology student and with ease descended to around 30 metres to collect some scallops for brood stock, without thinking too much more about it. I felt a little nervous at first, but it soon gave way to exhilaration. I loved the feeling of weightlessness, and exploring the strange underwater world was exciting and challenging at the same time.

Learning this new skill, and being able to dive alongside Nic, was wonderful, and during that period I felt my love of the sea deepen and diversify, in the same way that my love for Nic was intensifying with each day. As well as discovering a new facet of the sea, the element I loved so much, I felt that I was finding out more about myself too. I was incredibly proud that I was able to dive in spite of my fears, and it gave a tremendous boost to my confidence; it was all such fun.

While I soon learned to love diving, the best times were when Nic and I went down together, hand in hand, just the two of us. On one occasion, a plan was hatched to explore a submerged wreck in Blind Harbour; we were hoping to find gold. An air lift we'd made previously out of some Wavin pipe was assembled and we used this to excavate the site in our spare time, and we even got our hands on some spoils, the best being a gold button! Then there were the afternoons when we felt like having fresh seafood for supper, so we'd dive in the early evening, invariably bringing back at least a couple of dozen scallops to enjoy with a glass of wine. However, the biggest treasure was the shared wonder of what we'd witness together as we skimmed along the ocean bed with its interesting fish and other marine life.

I also enjoyed helping Nic out with the business. I'd always thrived when discovering new things and in new environments, so I relished the challenge of learning the lingo of the diving world and how it all worked, which would allow me to help out with Sundancer. I found the marine research work fascinating, particularly the bluefin project, and it wasn't long before I was making calls to coordinate the shipping of the huge tuna (each the size of an average human adult) from Belfast to Tokyo, including putting in orders for the carton 'coffins' in which the individual fish would be transported whole. Lauraine would laugh when she found me pacing up and down with the cordless phone cradled under my chin as I negotiated fiercely with some Japanese official on the other end of the line. With Nic in my life, it was always easy, even thrilling, to go beyond my comfort zone.

Eight

As I lie in limbo, in the anteroom between life and death, a vision comes to me. It will be one that stays with me for many years, and most likely for the rest of my life. I'm trying to pass through a door, a narrow wooden entrance that is sitting horizontally, on its side, right in front of me. I am vertical, upright, so I'm the wrong way round to be able to fit into the door; not only that, but my body is an amorphous yet solid mass, far too big and ungainly to pass through the space, even if the door was the right way round. But I ignore all of this and continue to try to force myself through the door. I am spent, and the very little will I have left is utterly focused on passing through and beyond the door.

All at once, beside me, I see a young black couple in old-fashioned dress. They are attractive and smiling, and a strong, benevolent energy emanates from them both. The young woman is wearing an Edwardian-style dress in black-and-white silk with a large bustle. Over the intricate bodice, she wears a black jacket in fine silk, and at her neck is a white lace ruffle. In one hand she is holding an elegant black-and-white silk parasol; on her head is a gorgeous black silk bonnet. The young man is also wearing black and white, a silk top hat with a beautiful sheen, a crisp white shirt and a morning suit and cape.

Now they are both watching as I try and try to force myself through the sideways door.

'Oh no, you can't go through there, honey,' the young woman says kindly. 'It's not your time.' I can hear the luxurious rustle of her dress as she moves forward and smiles.

'That's right,' the young man agrees, with a pleasing, warm smile. 'You can't get through there, don't you see, my dear? You'll never fit.'

They continue like this for a while, speaking in mellow, lilting American accents, as if gently amused by my efforts, trying to persuade me with kindness and quiet humour that I need to accept reality and give up my futile attempts to pass through the door. All the time they are smiling – beautiful, benevolent smiles radiating love and compassion. It feels like they know me, and love me, and want only what is best for me.

Then I'm at the very base of a tall, tall cliff, looking upwards. Suddenly I hear a voice – distant, thin – from far above.

'Rachel, we're going to have to operate again.'

Over and over, I can hear the words: 'We've got to operate again, we've got to operate again', and I realise with a shock that I've got to protest, to make myself heard. I desperately need to find my voice so that the people at the top of the cliff can make out what I'm saying.

I'm fighting hard to speak, but it feels impossible. I'm weak, weaker than I've ever been. My life force is depleted, and summoning the energy to speak feels like too big an ask. It would be so easy, so much easier, to just let myself go under.

My throat is constricted and I feel as if my heart is going to burst from sheer futility as I struggle to find and project my voice.

Panicking . . . I breathe . . . Then finally, with the very last vestiges of the air in my lungs and energy in my body, I manage to say:

'Don't, don't . . . I won't survive any more—'

And then, I'm done. I can let go and surrender; I can drift away at last.

◆ ◆ ◆

It was only much later, some weeks after surgery, that I would hear my mum's account of what had happened late in the evening after my surgery and make some sense of that strange, unforgettable vision I'd had in my unconscious state; the dream sequence so vivid it will stay forever with me. Every tiny detail is etched in my mind: the expressions on the faces of the young couple, their exact words, every nuance of what I was thinking and feeling from one moment to the next. Even today, as I write, I can see all of it again with astonishing clarity.

Mum and my brother Adrian arrived at the hospital some time after Mr Nelson had begun operating. I'd asked them not to plan to arrive earlier when I was still on the ward – I've no idea why, maybe another example of my determination to handle things on my own. Jane Gotto, who'd arrived separately, was allowed to wait with my mum and Adrian in a corridor near the operating theatre; they'd been told they could stay there for as long as they wanted to. They took it in turns to keep vigil in that corridor for the entire duration of my surgery, which would end up being close to fifteen hours.

Initially, Mum later recounted, every hour or so Richard Nelson would emerge from theatre to take a quick breather in the corridor and update them on what was happening. There were at least two other surgeons in attendance to assist him. My mum recalls how, as the hours passed, Richard began to look whiter and more tired each time he came out.

As the hours stretched into evening, these regular progress reports began to peter out, and Mum, Adrian and Jane just had to sit there, wondering what was happening and how I was faring. They'd fallen into complete silence by this time, too tired and worried to talk. By the tenth hour of surgery, with no news or updates for a long time, my mum's fear and uncertainty began to turn into hopelessness and the growing conviction that I couldn't possibly survive; she began privately to say goodbye and to resign herself to the idea she might never see me alive again.

And still the time passed, more and more slowly. Finally, around the fourteen-hour mark, Richard Nelson emerged, exhausted.

'Well, your daughter's still alive, Mrs Bendon – she's in recovery. We've no idea yet how things went, or how successful the operation has been, but we got it all – and we won't know anything more until Rachel begins to wake up. So for now, it's still just a waiting game. But I'll let you know as soon as there are any developments.' And with that, he turned around and walked back through the theatre doors.

Mum, Adrian and Jane felt an overwhelming sense of relief. Each one of them had privately feared the worst but hadn't wanted to share such thoughts with the others. However, as time began to go by once more, and everything was still silent, the anxiety began to creep back again. Why hadn't I come around by this time? Was I ever going to wake up?

Suddenly Richard Nelson was out of theatre again, looking strained.

'She is still unresponsive at this point, Mrs Bendon – and she should really have regained consciousness by now. We need to do another CT scan urgently, so that we can get a clearer sense of what is happening. Time really is of the essence now. I'll keep you informed.'

A short time later, he reappeared, his face drawn with fatigue and concern.

'I'm afraid the scan has shown that Rachel has an intracranial bleed. The bleeding is showing no signs of slowing down and, if it continues, it's going to create a build-up of pressure inside the skull, possibly causing brain damage. My feeling is that we will have to operate again, to save her life. I'm going back into the X-ray unit again now – we're keeping her in there so that we can monitor what's happening – to see if there are any developments. But I need to know now that, if I make the call that surgery is the only option, I have your permission to go ahead. Ideally we'd like to wait and see, but as Rachel's still unresponsive, we will probably just have to proceed regardless.' My family agreed immediately, knowing it was my only chance.

And then Richard Nelson disappeared again, leaving them distraught.

◆ ◆ ◆

'*We've got to operate again . . .*'

I don't know how, but these words must somehow have pierced my awareness, even as I lay in my unconscious state. I must have known then, subliminally, that death was close, and that all my energy was dissipating fast. To this day, I'm convinced that these critical life-or-death moments coincided exactly with the visitation of that young, beautiful couple from a bygone era. I genuinely believe it was their intervention, their insistence that I should not pass through the sideways door, that brought me back from the brink of death. The vision I had of them is what enabled me to articulate, with every ounce of strength I could muster, my certainty that I wouldn't survive having my head opened again at that critical juncture.

'Don't . . .'

It seems that a nurse who was standing close beside me as I lay in the CT scanning suite heard me say these words and alerted Richard Nelson and the other surgeons. At this possible sign of some responsiveness, he decided to give me a few more hours before taking me back into theatre. 'All we can do now is hope, and pray, that the bleeding stops,' he told everyone as they sat in the corridor in nervous dread, 'and that Rachel's brain begins to re-absorb the large clot which has been forming. After what she's already endured today, there's a high likelihood that she just wouldn't survive more surgery.' And with that, Mum, Adrian and Jane had to steel themselves for yet another agonising wait.

Some hours later, the bleeding in my brain did begin to slow down, and then it stopped altogether. Somehow, the potentially deadly clot began very gradually to break down and disperse itself. Later, the staff who had been observing me throughout this critical time would describe this development as being nothing short of miraculous. As for me, I will always believe that my life was in some way saved by the strange intervention of that young African-American couple from the turn of the last century.

73

Nine

Everything around me appeared upside down. It was the oddest experience. My eyes were so swollen that I could only open them by lifting up my lids with a shaky right hand, and just for a few moments at a time, so I could get snatched glimpses of the ward in which I now lay – but what I did see was topsy-turvy and made little sense. The nurses moving about were upside down, their feet where their heads should have been, and vice versa. Other patients nearby seemed to defy gravity, able to stay lying horizontal when they should rightfully have been falling to the floor from their upside-down beds.

It was hard to process, and hard to navigate too, once I needed to do so. In those first few days, I remember Nic's sister Sara spoon-feeding me mashed potato, and how the spoon seemed to be coming down at me from a great height. It was all very bizarre, but at the time I wasn't able to analyse it sufficiently to be able to ask someone why this was happening, or if it would always be like this.

Otherwise, I can remember very little about those initial days after surgery. I simply lay in my bed, drifting in and out of sleep, as if all my senses and mental processes were muffled in cotton wool. Everything felt blurry, indistinct. The doctors' main goal at this stage was to keep my brain as quiet as possible, to minimise all external and internal stimulation, in order to buy me some vital space to recover from the huge 'insult to the brain' caused by the surgery and then the intracranial bleed. And so, every time I began to stir even slightly from my semi-alert state, someone would top up my drip with another dose of phenobarbitone – an anti-seizure and sedative drug – and I'd sink once more into oblivion.

One source of considerable distress was a constant, searing pain in my right arm and shoulder. This, I later learned, was being caused by the nerve damage I'd suffered as a result of having my head and neck kept so tightly clamped and immobile during the fifteen hours of surgery. So in addition to the phenobarbitone, I was being given hefty doses of oral morphine, and the combined effect was a chemical cosh to my brain.

◆ ◆ ◆

Only a very short time later I had stabilised enough to be moved down to the High Dependency Unit (HDU) on the ward. Gradually, I was becoming more conscious and aware of my situation and surroundings. I felt like I was slowly emerging from a thick fog into a world that was more sharply defined and real. I can remember clearly the very moment when I first tried to galvanise my body into movement. My mental processes were still sluggish, but I went through the usual process of trying to stretch and turn over in the bed, but nothing much happened. What was wrong? I went to move again, pulling with my right leg and straining my neck to haul my body round and over. But again, nothing. There must be something weighing me down, I thought; I can't move my left side at all. That I could still feel the full length of my left leg, and the sheets resting on top of it, made it all the more puzzling. Panic flickered through my mind and I broke into a sweat. Could this be? It felt as if there were lead weights strapped to my left arm and leg, pinning me to the bed. I strained some more, but still nothing happened. Breathing heavily now, I felt the panic rising fast. Something was terribly wrong. The tears came and I called out: 'Nurse, nurse, please come!' I waited, my heart pounding. I couldn't bear any more.

Moments later, a ward nurse arrived.

'Everything okay, Rachel?'

'I don't know what's going on . . . I've just tried to turn over and I can't. I'm trying to move but my body won't work. Please, tell me, what's happening?' I pleaded, my voice rising in alarm.

She disappeared to find someone, and a short time later I saw my surgeon walking up the ward towards me (by this time, things no longer appeared upside down, which I suppose was at least something to be grateful for). As he approached, I found myself scanning his face for signs of concern or consternation. But his expression was impassive, neutral, as it generally was. I saw that he had someone with him – a younger guy, also wearing scrubs.

'Hello, Mrs Gotto. Good to see you looking much more alert . . . Let me introduce my colleague; he's just flown in from the States today to do some work with us here in Neurology.'

I glanced briefly at the younger man but quickly moved my attention back to Richard, looking at him expectantly.

'So,' he began, 'the nurses have told me what's been happening this morning. What you're experiencing now, Mrs Gotto, is a loss of movement as a result of your surgery. As you know, the op went as well as it could have, even with the complication of the bleed. We managed to successfully excise all of the tumour, and of course you're still with us and have managed to get through a very tough first few days on ICU. However, as we anticipated, the surgery looks like it caused some damage to the right pre-frontal cortex, in the motor centre of your brain – and this means that you now have paralysis on the left-hand side of your body. As I explained before, we can't know what exactly we have done to your brain during surgery, and we're only likely to know this, and the extent of it, with the passing of time and as you gradually regain function . . . or don't regain function, as the case may be.'

He paused, and I noticed him glance briefly at his colleague and then at the nurse who was standing at the side of my bed.

'Mrs Gotto, the paralysis may or may not be permanent. We don't know, and can't tell at this stage. I can't say with any confidence what your future will look like at this point.'

Meanwhile, I was silent. I'm not sure how much of this I was really taking on board. I do remember feeling panic and the pin-prick of tears, though this wasn't necessarily significant in itself. In those early days, like many people who have suffered brain damage, I would often find myself at the mercy of a series of intense emotional states over which I had absolutely no control. Especially at night in the HDU, I'd find myself weeping uncontrollably for hours, unable to stem the tears or make sense of my feelings. However, it's clear that Richard Nelson's words must have had some visible impact on me, which he could read from my expression.

'Look, I know it's a lot to take in, Mrs Gotto . . . So we'll leave you for a while. But do of course let any of us know if you have any questions. And please don't forget that it's very early days – very early indeed – and that some degree of recovery is still possible. Once you're feeling stronger, when the time is right, you'll go on to the Brain Injury Rehabilitation Unit. They'll be doing lots of rehab, which has had good results in many patients. Anyway, that's really all I can say for now. At this stage, it's very important for you to get as much rest as possible and allow your brain the time it needs to recuperate to the extent it can.'

After he left, I lay there, trying to absorb what he'd just said. I was unnerved by what, in that moment, felt like insurmountable obstacles. Being naturally left-handed, the paralysis of my left side meant that I'd lost the use not only of my left leg but of my dominant hand. Over the next few weeks, I had no choice but to begin using my right hand. Initially, doing anything for myself was practically impossible, quite literally. My right hand was shaky and weak and I was still in horrific pain due to the nerve damage I'd suffered during surgery. Brushing my teeth became a major affair. I remember trying to get the brush to meet my mouth, and the oddly disconcerting feeling as my motor skills simply wouldn't comply. The sheer difficulty of it was a real eye-opener and also frightening. How much would I have to learn? How would I manage? I felt a cold sense of dread. My future looked bleak. I wondered what the point of surviving all of this was, only to be left like this, broken.

◆　◆　◆

I spent a few days in the HDU, and as my condition continued to stabilise I was moved from a 'high obs' bed to one further down the ward. Although Richard Nelson had been extremely frank with me, I was still very slow to absorb what he said. That I was now completely dependent on others for the most basic things was clear. I had a catheter, and bedpans had to be brought to me. I was unable to move much without assistance, and still had to be spoon-fed and given bed baths by the nurses. So, I couldn't pee, empty my bowels, feed myself, wash or move without help, and was completely paralysed on the left-hand side, with limited use of my right hand and arm.

Never at any point, however, had I lost the ability to speak or to process language. From the outset, and even at the time of my diagnosis, this hadn't ever been cited as a possibility, as the AVM was not anywhere near the brain's speech centre. More than once, people (hospital staff and some friends and family members) mentioned how lucky I was in this regard, and while I knew they were only trying to be positive, I couldn't help replying with a touch of dry humour: 'Yes, you're right . . . but right now *this* is hardly something to celebrate, though, is it?' – and I'd cast a glance down at my inert body under the bedclothes.

Only once I was allowed very short visits from people beyond my immediate, very close circle did I truly begin to understand my situation. The shock and sorrow in their eyes when they first saw me were unmistakable. It was the sorrow above all that made me sad, because it made my situation real. To my very close family and friends, in spite of my predicament, I was still Rachel, to some degree anyway. But those who didn't know me as well couldn't disguise their shock when they saw me so helpless. Then I knew it: everything had changed radically. I was utterly dependent, my autonomy gone and, with it, my freedom. As I believed it then, from that moment I was to become chiefly an object of pity to the outside world. This was almost as much of a body blow as losing all movement on my left-hand side. Rightly or, no doubt, wrongly, I felt a deep, visceral sense of what I can only describe as humiliation at having to rely on others for everything, even my most basic physical needs. Yet I had no choice but to proceed with life, and without any appreciable sense of whether things would ever be any different.

Ten

Dominic died, you see. My dear brother, my childhood companion and sibling soulmate; my beautiful, smart, wild Dominic died. He was only twenty-eight years old. Like me, he loved the sea. He was a free spirit who left home when he was just eighteen, before doing his final school exams, and went on to make a living working on yachts and delivering them across the Atlantic. Among many other far-flung locations, he spent time in the Caribbean and then in the Canaries, where he met Lauraine.

Handsome, tanned, golden-haired Dominic was quick-witted and could be hilariously funny, often at the expense of others who hadn't been blessed with the kind of intelligence, looks and charm he had. Full of youth, physical confidence and bravado, he loved adventure and exotic places and people who shared his bohemian take on life. But he was also a deeply troubled man who would shrug off the attempts of those who loved him to keep him close. He could be impatient, intolerant and sometimes even actively cruel with me and, later as a young man, with the women who were drawn to him romantically, mesmerised by his mischievous smile and humour. He broke hearts without a second thought.

But he was my brother and I loved him without question. There was just over a year between us; he'd been born in March in 1968 and I in May 1969. We were inseparable as children; so close that even as a teenager and later as a young woman, I honestly wouldn't have been able to say where I ended and he began. It felt as if we were two parts of the same person. Having been a witness to his childhood, as he was to mine, I understood, deeply, the pain he carried at his core. I knew why he grew up to be so emotionally closed off, so off-hand and caustic, occasionally cold-hearted and, at times, so dismissive of me and of the other people who cared about him.

By the time we moved to 'the big house', our older brothers had all left home. As the remaining son – and one who was quickly growing into a strong, virile and handsome young man – Dominic in particular was the target of my father's vitriol. While I became more and more broken as the emotional dysfunction raged on, Dominic became more consumed with pent-up anger, in the way that thwarted, strong-willed young men tend to be. I remember that as a boy and then a teenager he frequently had problems with his stomach – and looking back, I can see how this makes perfect sense. To my mind, the constant stress and tension of living in that cold, oppressive house under my father's regime of tight control meant that my brother was always waiting for the next argument to erupt, always primed and on the alert.

By the time he was in his early twenties, and although he had some years earlier left home, Glandore and my father far behind, it seemed clear to those who knew Dominic well that he was eaten up by a deep emotional wound and was somehow convinced that there was something profoundly unlovable about him, something he felt was weak, defective. He had fully absorbed the pervasive sense of rejection and disdain which inhabited the air around him from very early on. Although he escaped as soon as he could, by then I believe immeasurable damage had been done, and neither the freedom of his years at sea nor the happiness of his time with Lauraine could fully erase it or enable him to love himself for the person that he was.

By February 1994, when Dominic brought Lauraine back to Glandore with him for the summer, he was showing early signs of being unwell. The problems with his stomach had been flaring up again. Dominic wasn't a great believer in conventional medicine or regular doctors. We had been taught not to trust them and, for a long time, he shrugged off our suggestions – mine, the family's and Lauraine's – that he should get himself checked out. Initially he insisted there was nothing to worry about, putting the resurgence of his symptoms down to the stressful trip he and Lauraine had just returned from, a yacht delivery that should have been a manageable undertaking but which had quickly turned into a disaster.

But when his symptoms didn't calm down, and only became increasingly uncomfortable and debilitating, Dominic finally agreed to see his doctor, who quickly referred him for a series of tests at the Bon Secours Hospital, Cork. He underplayed all of this to such an extent, however, that on the day he was due to collect the results from the consultant, no one felt it necessary to go with him. I still clearly remember that day. Lauraine and I had been working at the restaurant that afternoon, and he'd called in to see us on his way to the hospital. When we wished him luck, he was his usual nonchalant self, insisting there would be nothing to worry about. Only after much cajoling did he promise he'd let us know on his way home how it all had gone. He agreed to meet us at the pub where Lauraine and I were planning to have a drink after work.

In truth, I didn't give the matter much more thought for the rest of that day. It was a very busy afternoon in The Pier House and, in any case, Dominic had been so low key about everything that I wasn't particularly worried. My brother was a very fit, active twenty-six-year-old man: why on earth would there be anything seriously wrong with him?

But Dominic did call into the pub to see us when he got back, and much later than we expected. His face said it all.

'Dominic! So, how did it go?'

'I thought I'd just stop off at the flat first, and ended up doing a couple of things there without realising the time . . .' Since their return to Glandore, Dominic and Lauraine had been living in one of the flats in the courtyard of my mum's house overlooking Glandore Harbour. I'd been aware that they'd been having problems around this time – something to do with what had happened during the trip they'd recently come back from – but as far as I could see, they were still very much together as a couple.

'Right . . . okay. Well, anyway, what did the consultant say? Is everything all right?' I prompted him again. Although he didn't look upset, something about his manner was beginning to make me feel a gnawing, low-level anxiety.

'Uh, okay then. Well' – Dominic shifted a little as he stood there, then pulled out a stool from the bar to sit with us at the counter – 'he says it's bowel cancer.'

Eleven

The physical surroundings of the neurology ward certainly didn't help to create any sense of comfort or restfulness. Everything was functional, with absolutely no frills. Much of this was because the ward was housed in a former military hospital, with low ceilings, thin walls with no insulation and scant natural light. The space allotted to each bed was minimal, as if we were wounded soldiers in wartime.

After the HDU, I'd been returned to the same general neurology ward I'd been initially admitted to the evening before surgery. I was still on a number of heavy-duty medications, but I was becoming a good deal more lucid. It's a period I find myself reluctant to revisit, as it was very dark and painful.

The cold, especially, is something I'll never forget. Perhaps because of the paper-thin walls, it felt as if the patients spent much of the time shivering, which hardly seems appropriate, given the compromised immunity that goes with recovering from life-changing brain injury. Unbelievably, we had to take turns with the few extra blankets which seemed to be the limit of the bedding resources allocated to our ward. It was hard to reconcile all this with the fact that, at that time, this department was regarded as one of the UK's top centres for neurosurgery. And it made not a jot of difference that I was (by necessity) a private patient; there were certainly no added extras or perks.

Particularly at night, the routine of the ward was relentless, with neurological checks and obs religiously carried out every hour. This was crucially important for my care, but it made for constant wakefulness. The hours after midnight were also when I struggled most with waves of uncontrollable emotion. Perhaps there was something about the silent ward in the dimmed light which made me feel more isolated and desolate than I did during the day. Once the night staff came on duty, I would lie, weeping, for hours, interrupted only by the neuro obs. And while I was aware that other patients might hear me and be unsettled by it, I simply couldn't stop.

In fact, it wasn't other patients who were bothered most by my tears, but one particular nurse on the night shift, and she really scared me. About ten years older than me, she would come over to scold me and then laugh because I was crying: '*Stop* crying . . . Just stop!' When I tried to explain that I couldn't help it, she just looked at me coldly and brusquely walked away again, without another word. Then, ten minutes later, she'd come over again to tell me off. This was a nightly occurrence when she was on shift, and I quickly began to dread the times she'd be on duty.

It wasn't long before I was paranoid about who would be on the night shift. That nurse's ridicule scared me and made me feel vulnerable, and I just couldn't understand how she could be so cold. Neither did she seem to understand the well-documented difficulty that many brain injury patients have keeping their emotions in check. I began to live for the nights when she wasn't working, because the nurse who filled in for her was the diametric opposite. That your quality of life can turn on a knife-edge became all too apparent; everything depended on the mood and disposition of those tasked with your care.

I hated being so powerless. Simply resigning myself to an unsatisfactory or deeply distressing situation was utterly alien to me, as I'd always strongly believed in the power of self-determination. If I didn't like the circumstances I found myself in, I'd always find a way to summon the grit to create something better. The sense of disempowerment which defined my new reality was a source of deep confusion and frustration that I found nigh on impossible to come to terms with.

I decided, however, to tell my family and some of the staff about the abusive night nurse, but while my mum believed me, the others seemed to just shrug it off as nothing of importance. They were probably privately thinking that my judgement couldn't really be trusted, given my current state, or that I was merely venting. Perhaps they reckoned that it was the drugs talking, and not me.

Eventually, with my mum's help, I made a complaint, but nothing happened. Management seemed keen to downplay the situation and quietly brushed it under the carpet. No action was taken, and, if anything, my attempt to address the situation only made things worse. The nurse remained on her usual shifts, except now, I was sure I could detect an extra edge to her ridicule. She never directly addressed anything with me, but when she looked at me after that it was with undisguised contempt. The only blessing was that my stay on the ward was relatively short – about three weeks. I knew I was lucky not to be there as a long-term patient, but that's not how it felt at the time.

Thankfully, perhaps, during my time on the neurology ward I had continued to nurture some illusions about my situation. This is likely part of a natural psychological defence mechanism, where your mind protects you from too many glimpses into the reality of any sudden shocking change of circumstances. That I actively maintained a certain level of denial during those early days is borne out very clearly by a handful of key moments.

One afternoon, the nurses told me that the following day I'd be getting out of bed for the first time. Although this wasn't explicitly presented to me as progress, I felt that it most surely must be and, with some enthusiasm, I told my visitors all about it. Like me, they felt it must represent some kind of progress, but looking back, it's more likely that they were just humouring me.

By this stage, as some strength started to return, I'd been gradually adjusting to the transition from lying flat and unable to move to at last being able to 'sit up' with my head almost upright, although only with the support of several pillows. Even this progress had been painstakingly slow. Initially, raising my head above the horizontal had caused waves of nausea and vertigo. By the time I was told that I'd be 'getting out of bed', I was able to sit upright for periods of up to half an hour at a time before weakness forced me to lie flat again. But I hadn't regained any movement on my left side. How on earth, then, did I imagine I'd be able to get out of bed the next day? My denial today strikes me as almost comical, but at the time it felt far from funny.

The next morning, while Breeda was visiting, three nurses arrived to say that the time had come for me to get up – for the very first time. My initial sense of excitement very quickly turned to dismay when I saw that they had brought with them quite a collection of equipment. 'Okay, Rachel – we'll have you up and out of bed in a jiffy,' one of the nurses said cheerily, as she winked conspiratorially at Breeda.

Unfortunately, the tortuous process that unfolded next took far longer than 'a jiffy'. Firstly, a large canvas sheet was carefully manoeuvred under my inert body by a series of shifting movements, until finally I was lying fully on its surface. Then each of the sheet corners was attached to a hoisting device, and slowly,

slowly, I was winched upwards. Next, I was carefully guided over to a wheelchair and then painstakingly lowered into it in a sitting position. The canvas sheet was swiftly unhooked and removed, and all three nurses busied themselves placing my limbs in the desired position and securing each one to the arms and base of the chair by means of various straps and belts.

Almost as soon as I was 'up, out of bed for the first time', my dismay at all the palaver it had taken to get me there turned into vertigo and nausea.

'Oh God, I'm sorry . . . I think I'm going to . . . I'm going to have to go back to bed, right now. Please!' I gasped, beginning to sob. My muscles were far too weak, my sense of balance far too compromised.

'Ah now, don't worry, love. It happens a lot, the first time especially. We'll get you straight back into bed. You can just take it easy. We'll try again tomorrow. You'll get used to it in no time, you'll see.'

I knew instinctively that it would take far longer than 'no time' before I'd get used to sitting upright in the wheelchair. Once more I felt overwhelmed with despair, as I looked first at the nurses and then at the discarded equipment around my bed. Meeting Breeda's gaze, I couldn't fail to see the tears filling her eyes, and my heart sank. I wasn't really getting up, at least not in the way I'd fooled myself into thinking.

While all of this had been going on, my dear friend had simply stood there as a shocked witness. I've always loved Breeda's unwillingness to buy into the 'bullshit' of others or put on a public face just because it's what is expected of her. With Breeda, what you see is what you get. Seeing my helplessness and humiliation, she couldn't hide the pain she felt on my behalf.

Many years later, Breeda would tell me what she was thinking during this episode. I could have guessed myself but, nevertheless, it made me shiver. 'When I saw you that day – the way you

88

were, how they had to manhandle you – I couldn't bear it. In that moment I honestly wished that you had died in surgery, Rachel. That's not what, or who, you were born to be . . . So much so that I just didn't want you to survive. That's why I was crying.'

This broke my heart, not just because of what she'd said and thought but because for a moment, all this time later, I felt a deep sense of compassion for myself. I'd gone through most of that period in a daze, and finally my heart broke for my experiences, and I was glad.

Twelve

The months following Dominic's diagnosis were a terrible, bitter-sweet rollercoaster, as I veered uncontrollably between deep anguish and heady, almost unreal joy. The news that, at twenty-six years old, my beloved brother had bowel cancer hit me like a ton of bricks and left us all reeling. Yet I'd only just met Nic, the man I knew I wanted to spend my life with and who'd also turned my life upside down, but in such a very different way. I can honestly say I've never felt so torn; between two lives and two states of being – falling in love and being in shock – and between two men who each in their own way needed me with an urgency that couldn't wait.

On the one hand, my heart was broken at the idea that Dominic potentially might not survive; on the other, the joy I'd found with Nic flooded my soul with love, light and a feeling of at last coming home. At times I felt I would fall apart with the sheer effort of trying to contain so many conflicting emotions, and of trying to do all the things I felt desperately needed my attention. Nic was wonderful, so supportive and kind and understanding of my drive to do everything within my power to help my brother. Ultimately, although in truth there was little he or I or any of us could do, I knew that for as long as Dominic was with us I had to try.

From the start his doctors had been adamant that the best course of action – the only thing that would buy him more time, if not perhaps bring about an improvement or cure – was immediate surgery, followed by aggressive chemotherapy. An inevitable consequence of the surgery would be that he'd need to have a stoma and a colostomy bag fitted, permanently. This is very difficult for anyone to contemplate, let alone an active man in his twenties, yet it was just one of the many factors that played into Dominic's absolute refusal to go down the route his medical team were proposing, or indeed to consider any other conventional treatment options. The main reason behind his decision, however, was his firm belief that alternative medicine could be just as if not more powerful and effective than anything mainstream medicine had to offer.

This wasn't just a sudden whim or notion on my brother's part. It was consistent with a general philosophy about health and lifestyle which he had subscribed to for a long time (even though, until then, some aspects of his own lifestyle didn't always reflect these beliefs!). I know that he was greatly influenced in this thinking by our upbringing. My father and mother were both very much ahead of their time as proponents of organic produce in the 1960s, and when they came to Ireland just before I was born they bought land which they operated as a self-sufficient concern, growing vegetables and fruit, keeping goats and hens for milk and eggs, and supplementing our diet with fish and other seafood from the local waters. They believed that an outdoorsy, healthy lifestyle and a natural, unprocessed diet were the keys to health and longevity. Dominic had always had a lot of time for these ideas. He had also absorbed, subconsciously, my father's belief that we all had the power to heal ourselves better than any doctor. It's no surprise, then, that Dominic was convinced that conventional medicine wasn't always the best recourse at times of ill health and that he could heal his cancer by other means.

In the initial period after his diagnosis, he eschewed conventional treatments and embarked on the search for a cure by exploring alternative approaches. In the first instance, he sought the assistance of the renowned naturopathic nutritionist John Garvey, based in West Cork, to help him devise a dietary regime that would maximise his chances of recovery. Dominic also immediately gave up smoking and drinking alcohol and began a rigorous yet restorative exercise programme and a visualisation programme – all of which, his thinking was, would ensure that his immune system was as strong as possible in fighting the cancer. For a number of months, he stuck religiously to this regimen, convinced that this was the best way to at least stop the cancer in its tracks, if not eradicate it altogether. John Garvey's steady, strong support at this time helped Dominic tremendously, psychologically and otherwise.

Meanwhile, those of us who were close to him were struggling. Lauraine, who loved him intensely, was utterly distraught when he called time on their relationship shortly after his diagnosis. Things had been rocky between them for a while, since before they had come back to Glandore, but regardless of that, she was very much in love with him, and desperate to support him now that he was ill; she felt that any issues they had in their relationship should be set aside for the time being so that they could both focus completely on his recovery. But Dominic was insistent that it was over and that he didn't want to be with her any more. My own thinking then, and it hasn't changed much since, was that Dominic couldn't bear to let anyone love him in any circumstances, because of his own self-loathing, which told him that he wasn't worthy of love, especially that of such a good-hearted person as Lauraine. He couldn't bear to be vulnerable with her, and so the thought of Lauraine looking after him when he was ill – especially with such a visceral, undignified condition as bowel cancer – was completely intolerable for him. So he felt he had to be the one to put a stop to their relationship and create as much distance as he could between them. He agreed they could continue to live together until Lauraine could find somewhere else – after all, he did still care about her – but it must have been excruciating for them both, especially for her, to be at such close quarters yet emotionally so far apart.

From the day of his diagnosis, I was determined to channel all of my time and energies into Dominic's recovery. Not long afterwards, I gave up running the restaurant so that I could focus solely on being with my brother: getting him to his various appointments, helping him stick to his self-devised treatment regime and trying to keep up his morale. Along with our mother, I also spent many hours tirelessly researching alternative therapies and their possible efficacy in Dominic's situation. It wouldn't be an exaggeration to say that I quickly became immersed in helping my brother. The only thing that could divert my attention was time with Nic, and that was because we were still in the first throes of falling in love. When Nic and I were together, I got some respite from the constant thoughts, the ongoing, relentless anxiety and guilt about Dominic's illness.

The truth, so clear to me now, was that I was utterly co-dependent with Dominic. In part this was because we were so close, having spent every waking moment together as children. More than that, though, my own sense of self was so unformed and so bound up with self-questioning that I didn't know where I ended and he began. I was so accustomed to trying to keep others happy – doing whatever it took to get someone else's approval, or at least to escape their disapproval – that I believe I'd no idea who I was, or who I was without Dominic. When he became seriously ill, I was, therefore, consumed by guilt and by the oppressive, ever-present conviction that it was my responsibility, and mine alone, to make sure he got better. I wished that I had been the one to get cancer, so that he wouldn't have it; I was convinced I would be better able to handle it than he possibly could, because I sensed that I was stronger than him – and possibly also because somehow I deserved to be sick, whereas he didn't.

◆ ◆ ◆

After five or six months of following his diet- and exercise-based treatment programme, Dominic was massively discouraged when the latest tests showed the cancer was still actively progressing. In his disappointment, he became angry, filled with anxiety and resentment, a lot of which he directed at me and Lauraine, and often the family. Even worse, he became withdrawn and listless, sinking into depression and refusing to engage with anyone or anything. Desperate to turn this around, we went into overdrive with my research to see if we could find help further afield. I was going to do everything to make sure he got it, including travelling halfway across the world, if that's what it took. Even though at this point my mum was looking after my father full-time – now in his eighties, he was bedridden and partially paralysed after a catastrophic stroke – she joined me in researching every possible avenue in the hope of finding viable treatment for her beloved youngest son.

And for the next twelve months or so, this in effect is what we did. Dominic and I travelled the world in search of a cure.

I gave up my livelihood, the bistro business I'd put so much work and time and hope into; I even had an abortion, the first time I became pregnant by Nic, because my first and only priority was to rescue my brother. These were not carefully considered decisions; my decision-making was reckless, impulsive – something that was stronger than me and not susceptible to reason. I couldn't make any

94

distinction between myself and Dominic; I was him, he was me, and I had no identity independent of my brother.

Our first port of call was Mexico and the Oasis of Hope Hospital in Tijuana, right on the border with the US. It was my mum who had suggested it, after some weeks of research in the wake of Dominic's diagnosis. The hospital had been founded by the late Dr Ernesto Contreras, a distinguished physician who also conceived of a healing tradition known as the 'Total Cancer Care Approach', and today, the organisation is presided over by his son, distinguished surgeon and oncologist Dr Francisco Contreras. In the fifty-six years of its existence, the Oasis of Hope has become renowned for combining alternative medical approaches and conventional medicine within a framework of emotional and spiritual support to ensure the most effective possible treatment for its patients. Some of the alternative treatments offered include metabolic therapy, ozone therapy, pancreatic enzyme therapy, vitamin C megadoses and B-17 infusions; many of the approaches used are informed by the central tenets of the new science of epigenetics, which, in very simple terms, proposes that not everything in our genes is predetermined and that the environment in which we bathe our cells can be the pivotal difference between good health and ill health. Although some of these ideas and treatments were considered too experimental to be approved by the US medical authorities – hence the location of the clinic over the Mexican border – the hospital had had many successes with its treatment programmes, even in patients with Stage Four cancers.

Much of the hospital's philosophy struck a chord with Dominic's own ideas around health, so he decided he wanted to seek treatment there. And it seemed a foregone conclusion that I would be the one to accompany him. So we set out for Mexico, and Tijuana, without delay. I remember how on the flight there – from New York to San Diego – Dominic got outrageously drunk, despite the fact that he'd been abstaining from alcohol; he got quite out of control, shouting and acting out. I was mortified and at the same time deeply upset for him. I knew he must be terrified.

For our initial period in Tijuana, we stayed in a hotel, with Dominic going into the hospital every day for consultations and treatments and only returning late in the evening. After a while, however, it was clear that he was becoming very ill and he was admitted as a full-time in-patient. While he was very cooperative with the doctors and fully on board with the various therapies they tried, he was also angry and fed up, naturally enough, especially as it seemed that the cancer was continuing its relentless march forward. He took a lot of his anger out on me, and this only served to increase my burden of guilt: why had it not been me? I absorbed his frustration and pain and, even more than this, I accepted it as part of the role I'd always played when we were together. If he was angry, I was acquiescent and guilty; my poor Dominic.

I was a lost soul myself at that time. Every day I spent hours at the hospital getting to know the other patients and their families, seeing many of them succumbing to their illnesses. I would then spend solitary evenings in my hotel room, where I'd think obsessively about Dominic. My anxiety was such that I could barely eat or sleep, and I spent much of my time chain-smoking, with calls down to reception most nights for my usual order, '*Dos cerveza, por favour.*' In the days before mobile phones and cheap international calls, I wasn't able to talk to anyone from home, including Nic. Aside from people at the hospital, I wouldn't have thought to try to connect with anyone else in Tijuana, or in the neighbourhood, which at the time was a very tough area and the wrong place for a young woman unfamiliar with the city to be walking around at night on her own. I hadn't failed to notice the sturdy bars on the window of my hotel room; neither could I be unaware of the fear I felt even on my daily short walk to the hospital. Especially when one day, very early on in our stay, a huge 1970s American saloon-like car slowed to a crawl beside me and someone reached out of the window and yanked hard on my hair. I was ever vigilant after that.

Dominic was offered many treatments at the Oasis of Hope: apricot seed extract therapy (laetrile), IV infusions of vitamin C, the Warburg therapy, Lugols solution, nutraceuticals, vitamin K-3, organic vegetarian meals and juices, and so on. While these approaches had apparently been successful with other patients, it seemed that his condition was only worsening. In fact, as we approached the end of our month-long stay in Mexico, it became obvious that my brother was becoming too ill to be able to tolerate the journey back to Ireland so soon. Meanwhile, I was finding things very tough and, in many ways, I can see now that I was on the very edge of a nervous breakdown, I was so worn out both emotionally and physically. So we agreed with our family that my brother Nicky would come out to Tijuana for a time and I would return home as planned, with Nicky bringing Dominic back as soon as he was able to make the journey, which would be some days later.

In spite of how much time we spent together during his illness, Dominic and I never talked directly about his cancer, or about any prognosis he might have. We discussed at length the many details of the various treatments he tried; we talked about other possibilities yet to be explored and alternative places to which we could still go; we talked about anything and everything – when he wasn't too ill or too angry for conversation. But we never broached the possibility that we might not find a cure, or talked about what would happen if we didn't, or his thoughts or feelings about any of this. Neither of us had the language or the emotional insight to be able to directly confront the possibility that he might die, and we were so very young.

After some time back in Glandore, we rallied ourselves for more travel. By this time we had discovered Pascal Carmody's clinic in Killaloe, County Clare. Carmody had some very innovative cancer treatments available that he'd trained in and brought to Ireland from Germany. Over the course of a few months, Dominic and I spent five days a week in Killaloe during which he received the various treatments offered, returning to Glandore at the weekends. Things were becoming so exhausting for Dominic and, finally, as he wasn't responding in any meaningful way to his treatments, Pascal suggested that we should go to Germany and seek help at a specialist alternative cancer hospital there that he recommended.

And this we did. We went to Germany and the renowned Leonardis medical clinic in Kornwestheim, near Stuttgart. Again, Mum and I had done a great deal of research about the clinic in the preceding weeks and knew that the Leonardis Clinic had had great success with tumours such as prostate, breast, lung and colon cancers, as well as non-Hodgkin lymphoma. They also treated cancers of the skin, stomach/intestines, pancreas, ovaries, uterus, kidney, liver and brain, as well as leukaemia. As at the Oasis of Hope, their approach was holistic, aiming to treat the whole person rather than just the disease, and the range of treatments offered combined standard conventional therapies (chemotherapy, surgery, radiation) together with natural treatments and psychological therapies, including 'psycho-oncological' care, which involved various talk therapies and psychological support.

Dominic and I made a total of three trips to Kornwestheim over the months that followed, each time staying for several weeks. The surroundings and accommodation of the Leonardis Clinic were certainly much more congenial and, I felt, conducive to a health cure than the situation, at least in terms of location, of the Oasis of Hope. The clinic was located in a nice area within a nice town. Each patient had a shared room with en suite bathroom and all the facilities of a full-on hospital, but it was designed a bit more like a hotel so it simply didn't have that clinical coldness that most hospitals do.

And yet, in spite of all the treatments, Dominic continued to deteriorate. Each time we would embark on a journey to a new place, or discover a new therapy, he would feel a resurgence of hope and a rebooting of physical energy which that fresh hope inspired – for a short time, anyway. But each time we hit another dead end a sense of despair would set in again; and it was getting more and more difficult to sustain a positive attitude and to revive our faith in a cure.

As it turned out, it was one of Dominic's doctors in Germany who eventually had to spell things out for us, although in a manner that at least on the surface seemed rather cruel. Then again, perhaps he felt that neither Dominic nor I would have been able to deal with a more direct approach. We had been planning another trip to Stuttgart – our fourth – but Dominic was too sick to travel at all by this time, and we'd had to contact the clinic several times to postpone our arrival. At this point, Dominic's German doctor took it upon himself to send a letter to the consultant oncologist we were still in touch with at the hospital in Cork, but he chose to send the correspondence via Dominic, knowing of course that he would read it.

I can still clearly remember the day that letter arrived, and how Dominic, loath to open it himself, silently passed the envelope to me and asked me to read out what the doctor had written.

'. . . *Perhaps it would be better if Mr Bendon was allowed to fall into a coma and die . . .*' The typed words screamed up at me, hitting me with a force that left me unable to breathe.

'So, what does it say, Rach? Tell me!'

'Oh, Dominic, I'm so sorry . . .' I couldn't bring myself to read the words out loud. But I didn't need to; the expression on my face, the quietness of my voice, said it all. And no doubt Dominic had known the truth himself, deep down, for a very long time.

'It's okay . . . I tried,' was the only thing he said before turning to the wall. I felt as if I would collapse. Had it really come to this? There must be something else. What would become of us both now?

And with that, it felt as if the last vestiges of hope were gone. From that point onwards, it was evident that something in Dominic's energy had shifted; he no longer had the will to keep resisting his illness and what he now believed was its inevitable conclusion.

That is not to say, now that he had let go, that his death was an easy or mercifully quick process. It wasn't. Instead, it extended for many agonising weeks: the slow decimation and cruel dwindling of an energy and the very visceral disintegration of a young man's once virile body. Dominic was adamant that he wanted to die at home, and I was honour-bound to make this possible. Mum and I were to be his main carers. My own doctor, concerned about whether I'd be able to cope, questioned this decision, impressing on me how difficult things might get, but to my mind, there was no discussion to be had.

We nursed Dominic in his courtyard flat on my parents' property, with our local doctor paying regular visits to provide palliative care, including upping his morphine doses as required. For those of us who loved him, especially for my mother, it was excruciating to see his final, slow decline.

And yet during this time we also witnessed something else, something I can hardly express. The sicker my brother's body got, the lighter his energy, his soul, seemed to become. While the physical strain he endured became ever more oppressive, it felt as if a weight had been lifted from him and that his spirit was finally free, accepting, disconnected from the physical pain, and profoundly loving, even. He was able to tell the hospice nurse that he wasn't afraid of dying. Seeing my mother's pain, he asked her to promise to do something for him – to set about cultivating the walled garden beyond the nearby courtyard, which had lain fallow for years, with all the flowers and shrubs she loved so that we would have something to remember him by. He insisted that she start on the project straight away, while he was still with us, and she did so, taking time away every now and again from her vigil at his bedside, and over those weeks we could all see how this gave her some respite at least from the pain of watching her son die.

Dominic also spent increasing periods of time in conversation with the Reverend Richard Henderson, then the new Dean of Rosscarbery, who came to visit him on a regular basis. Initially these visits had been initiated by Richard, as part of his pastoral duties in his new parish, but soon it was Dominic who was actively requesting to see the young clergyman. This intrigued us, as Dominic had never been someone for religion or, as far as we knew, held any strong spiritual beliefs. And yet Richard was able to tell us, if not the exact content of these exchanges, that he had learned more from my brother during the time at his bedside than in all his years studying and practising his creed. He had come to my brother to bring spiritual solace, and yet it was Dominic who had new insights to bring to him.

Dominic died on 11 November 1996, Armistice Day. He was a spirited, wonderful, wild and deeply troubled soul, full of contradictions and complexity. It is over two decades since he left us, yet in so many ways it feels like yesterday. The 'what ifs' will resound for ever.

Thirteen

February 2006

Although my progress during my time on the neurology ward seemed agonisingly slow, each day I was growing a little stronger. I was becoming more accustomed to the whole routine of 'getting up' and sitting in the bedside chair for longer periods without immediately pleading to be put back into my bed. It's possible that now that I knew what was involved, it merely seemed less of a struggle.

A much more enjoyable 'first' was being able, finally, to have a shower. After wheeling me into the ward's purpose-built bathroom area, my nurse stationed me in one of the walk-in showers, took off my robe and went through the laborious process of soaping me down and rinsing me. The blissful sensation of warm water coursing over me, and of having shampoo massaged into hair that was matted and rancid after weeks of not being washed, was enough to take my mind off my predicament for a short time. But I couldn't allow myself to think of the sea, and how much I'd loved diving and swimming in the wild, salty water. As at other times in my life when full-frontal reality seemed overwhelming, I somehow instinctively knew that to think too far ahead would have been unbearable.

One of the most difficult things was the ongoing, relentless lack of personal space and privacy and, soon, I began to covet the one private room on the ward. The nurses told me that it could be taken only by patients who didn't need close observation on an ongoing basis, and that any occupant would simply stay until they were well enough to leave. So I was the first to notice one day when a patient was moved out.

Determined to seize my opportunity, I called over one of the nurses and asked if the last patient had completely vacated the room and when she replied that he had I immediately questioned whether I might be able to take the room for myself. Nervous that someone else might have had their eye on it, I hastily mentioned that I was improving every day and, on top of that, I reminded her that I had in fact had to pay for my own hospital stay, and was there was any way she could put a word in for me to get that single room? I'm quite sure the nurse could hear the desperation in my voice, and she replied that it wasn't up to her who got what room, and that I would need to be assessed by OT first, but she assured me that she would bring the subject up with the Nurse Manager at the next hand-over meeting.

She was true to her word, and the next day the ward sister came to say they'd be assessing my case as soon as possible. So I was over the moon when I was eventually told that yes, I was well enough, and they'd be moving me later that afternoon.

This simple change made a big difference to my quality of life on the ward: 'A crumb becomes a feast to a starving man,' as the saying goes. Although my door was kept open at all times so that staff could keep an eye on me, even that little bit of extra personal space and privacy made me feel slightly more like myself again.

Around this time, something happened which seemed to herald a big step forward. My mum had been to visit me and had just left the room to get her taxi. On her way out, however, she realised that she'd left her purse on my bedside table and so she came back to retrieve it.

'Rachel! I can't believe it,' she suddenly exclaimed as she came in.

'What's up, Mum?!' I was slightly alarmed by her tone.

'Rachel – your big toe just moved! The big toe on your left foot . . . Oh my God, I don't believe it . . . I'm going to call one of the nurses – they have to come and see this!' She hit the call button.

'Really – are you sure?' I hadn't been aware of anything myself, although I still had full sensation on my left side, in spite of the paralysis. My first thought was that it might just be wishful thinking on Mum's part.

'Yes, I'm absolutely sure. One hundred per cent. I just saw that toe move!'

When one of the nurses came into the room, however, she didn't seem to share our excitement. In fact, she was distinctly underwhelmed.

'Ah, okay . . . Well, these things can happen at this stage, you may occasionally experience involuntary twitching or jerking in the muscles, but it generally doesn't tend to signify anything in particular, you know.'

'But Rachel's big toe, on the paralysed side, actually moved . . . That must mean something, surely? That she's getting some movement back . . . ?' Mum insisted.

'That's not necessarily the case. It's not a good idea to jump to conclusions, no matter how much we all want something positive. But I tell you what, if it happens again, I'll be sure to let one of the doctors know.'

'Okay,' conceded my mum, clearly deflated. 'Though I still think it would be worth telling them now.'

A day or so later, as part of his regular daily rounds, Richard Nelson called into my room, once more accompanied by his younger American colleague. After the usual questions about how I was feeling, and after he'd checked my obs charts, medication and so on, he broached the 'toe development'.

'So, I believe you've experienced some movement on your left side. This is definitely worth keeping an eye on, but it's important not to get your hopes up. It could easily be a one-off, the result of a random muscle spasm. These can occur sometimes in patients at your stage after surgery.

'As I told you very early on, it's very possible that you will never regain any significant amount of mobility on your left side – you certainly won't ever recover full function in your left leg or be able to walk normally, without some kind of assistance. You shouldn't expect to be anywhere other than where you are now. So I brought your latest scans here with me today, just so that you can have a look.' He brandished a large envelope, out of which he slid yet another transparent image of my brain.

'If you look – here – you can see the area where the AVM was removed.' Even though I'd been shown similar scans since my operation, I was still shocked to see the large dark shadow – about a quarter of the area of my brain, it seemed – where there was no longer any grey matter or brain tissue, in effect, the gap where the AVM had been. It certainly brought home to me once more the extent of the trauma I'd suffered.

'Mrs Gotto, I'm not trying to be negative or discouraging, as I hope you know by now. I just need you not to have unrealistic expectations that might in the long term end up holding you back from adapting well and making the most of the positive aspects of your situation. You really have been doing very well, you know, in terms of regaining strength and already being able to do the things you can now do. And we'll continue to monitor any further developments with your toe, of course.'

After a few further pleasantries, he and his colleague left. As I lay there, I questioned the point of giving me so much information that I hadn't necessarily asked for. As someone who has always found it difficult to accept limitations being imposed on me and my life by others, especially those that seemed imposed just for the sake of it, I struggled now to take in what I was being told. It felt like all I had to look forward to was a future of chronic disability with very restricted possibilities.

Fourteen

As I approach the entrance of the tiny, beautiful church in Glandore on this, to all intents and purpose, the happiest of days, and see everyone assembled in the rows of pews, out of the blue the realisation hits me again that it is only a short year since we were all gathered in another church nearby, the previous November, for Dominic's funeral.

Naturally, I'd reflected on the anniversary and imagined I could anticipate and somehow short-circuit the flashbacks and the flood of sadness. But by then I was only learning how grief works – how it can knock you off your feet, often just when you thought you had it all neatly boxed off. So when Richard, the Dean, very kindly leans over to see if I would like some mention of Dominic during the service, grief hits and suddenly I feel as though I'm going to howl. I'm overwhelmed; perhaps it's far too soon. I miss Dominic like I miss a part of me. Again, I feel deep, wrenching guilt – that I'm alive and in love, and Dominic is dead. I just want to run out of the church – to go home, get into bed and give in to the pain I'd been so desperate to keep under control. Then I look at Nic and, though I'm exhausted and conflicted, I try to settle myself. You see, my grief wasn't the only thing weighing heavily on me that morning, but only two other people in the church knew what was going on.

As people toasted us after the blessing and settled at the garlanded tables of The Rectory to hear the speeches, Lauraine and her new boyfriend, Tim, were the only people aware that Nic and I had not signed our civil marriage certificate the day before, as planned. Everyone believed they were gathering together on our 'big day' to see our marriage blessed and help us celebrate. As anyone would, they assumed that all the formalities had been dealt with at our registry office ceremony the previous day and that, legally, we were already man and wife.

But when we arrived at the church, Nic and I weren't married. It was all entirely my fault. I'd forgotten to confirm the booking for our civil ceremony at the registry office some six weeks earlier, and when we turned up on what we believed was our civil wedding day, with Lauraine and Tim as our witnesses, we were sent away by the registrar, as no one had been expecting us and so another couple had been allotted our spot! Nor could they give us another date until well after the church ceremony in Glandore.

I can still feel my disbelief and horror at hearing the clerk say we couldn't be married that day. Immediately I thought of all the people who, right this minute, would be arriving in Glandore to celebrate our marriage the next day, after such a tragic family loss only one year before. They would be flying in from all over Europe to witness us pledge our lives to each other. What would we say if we didn't go ahead?

Leaving the registry office in shock, the four of us walked the short distance to a quiet pub just behind the courthouse and sat in silence, not knowing what to do or say. Then slowly, with the gentlest of smiles and looking me softly in the eye, Nic went down on bended knee on the pub's dirty, beer-stained carpet, slipped the gold wedding ring I was to wear on to my ring finger, and then asked me to do the same for him. He then kissed me tenderly and, rising from his knees, said, 'There, we are married and the show will go on.' I looked at him through my tears and began to protest that I didn't want to lie; I just couldn't. Lauraine and Tim, who agreed with Nic, took it in turns to convince me that it had to be done this way; besides, we had a new date to be married that was only four weeks away, and no one would find out. I felt so bad, as though I was being asked to play a part in a massive charade. My instinct was to come clean and tell everyone my mistake, and it took a few brandies and a lot of cajoling before they finally persuaded me that keeping quiet was the best option. Nic was adamant that in spirit we were married anyway. And so I finally gave in and we set off, back to West Cork, with our secret in tow.

On our 'wedding day', sworn to secrecy by Nic, I struggled with a niggling guilt, knowing that we wouldn't in fact formally marry for another four weeks. Years later, after Nic's death, when I told my mother-in-law the whole sorry story, she made me feel so much better when she said, 'You were married by God in the church that day and the rest was only a formality.' Phew!

Nic and I broke with tradition and arrived together at the church for our blessing. Side by side, we took our seats at the top of the church, and in front of family and friends our rings were blessed. It was a beautiful ceremony, and the overwhelming sense of connection and the rightness of it all swept me up in a radiant energy, so all at once there wasn't room to think of anything else, even my beloved Dominic. At last I could allow myself to become completely immersed in this moment, our day of commitment, when this wonderful man and I pledged our love for each other in front of all our friends and family members.

In the painful months since my brother's death, Nic had been my one steady, unfailing source of support. He held me close during the countless nights when my tears fell endlessly and my body ached with grief. He had tried to distract me with planning trips and filling our lives with warmth and closeness. He had cared for and loved me as no one else had ever done. So now, I was determined to set my sadness aside, for a time anyway, and focus all my attention on the joy of this day.

We wouldn't actually get married until we came back from our honeymoon in the Himalayas, in December 1997. That we had to live a lie of sorts in the intervening time was something we chose to accept. I wasn't able to fully relax until we touched down again in Cork airport, when we'd rushed to the registry office on our way home and officially got married in our travelling clothes, with Tim and Lauraine as our witnesses. Once we were pronounced man and wife for real, I breathed a huge sigh of relief. Finally, I could allow myself to feel the joy and the experience of being a happily married woman.

Very soon into the New Year of 1998, I learned that I was pregnant. It hadn't been part of our immediate plan. I'd wanted to wait a little longer, thinking it would be better to have more time to come to terms with Dominic's death, especially as it was only in the months that followed that I'd realised just how spent, physically and emotionally, I was after the endless travelling and search for treatment. However, once my pregnancy had been confirmed, I was very excited, and Nic was absolutely over the moon. After all the sorrow and struggle and exhaustion of the years of my brother's illness, it seemed that at last, my life might have turned a corner, and at the beginning of 1998 I remember feeling a little growing spark of curiosity and joy about what the future held.

Fifteen

By early spring, I was getting stronger and I had recovered sufficiently to be considered fit enough to go on to the next stage. This
meant a transfer to the Brain Injury Rehabilitation Unit – uni-
versally known as 'the BIRU' – a specialist treatment facility that
patients with acquired brain injuries moved to once they no longer
needed intensive nursing care. And it was when I was transferred
there that I encountered the infamous Pippa again.

'You're Pippa, aren't you?' I said to the girl as we were being
taken by our respective carers into the recreational area. I was in
my wheelchair, and this girl, my fellow patient, was being guided
by the arm as she walked slowly along.

'Yes, I'm Pippa – what's your name?'

It was hardly the most auspicious start to a conversation, but at
least it was a vast improvement on our very first encounter, when
she'd threatened to kill me. Yes, now that I was right up beside her,
I was able to confirm that it was indeed Pippa, the first patient I'd
met in the Frenchay on the eve of my surgery all those weeks ago –
the same girl who had been wheeled into the ward, bald and seeth-
ing, and who shouted that she would do something murderous if

she ever got her hands on me. And now we were both in the BIRU together, having been transferred there from the neurology ward.

As I told her my name, I also shared with her how we had first met. At that point I remember feeling kind of amused at the irony of us meeting up again, and therefore I felt really bad as a look of absolute horror and disbelief crossed her face at what I was saying. By her reaction, I could tell she simply had no idea what I was talking about. Her face said it all in that moment and, not wanting to make her feel any worse, I downplayed slightly how her threatening behaviour had affected me. It was clear also, by her reaction, that Pippa must have been very ill indeed at the time to have behaved as she did, because the woman I had just met appeared to be quite meek and mild. Instantly, I regretted blurting anything out, but it was too late, and she wanted to know everything that had happened, and so, quietly, I told her the whole saga from start to finish.

Pippa was shocked, and very upset.

'Oh my God, I never did that, did I? I don't remember anything at all, I'm so sorry. Since my op I have near complete amnesia. I'm so sorry, I didn't mean it, I'm sure. You know, I've kind of lost it these days, with all this stuff that's happened to my head and the surgery and that . . .'

Pippa truly looked a sorry sight as she sat beside me, her big eyes full of confusion. Scrutinising her a bit more, I noticed there wasn't much of her, in fact. I noted that she really was a very slight woman, small-boned, almost whippet-like, and privately I reckoned that had I been able to stand I would likely have towered over her. In reality, she seemed so fragile compared to my relative robustness, which was a bit ironic, given that I couldn't walk or stand, but her obvious mental fragility made me feel sorry for her.

In the end, I was genuinely pleased to see Pippa again, especially now that she seemed, and indeed looked, so much better and less hostile. There were certainly no airs and graces about her, though. She was tough, a little rough around the edges, but she was also a fellow survivor, someone who'd been through the 'neuro mill', as I had, and who was still here, so it felt like we had something very important in common. Even at that stage, however, I couldn't have guessed that within the space of the few short weeks to come we'd garner something akin to a friendship and that we'd help each other enormously in our respective processes of recovery.

◆ ◆ ◆

Being admitted to the BIRU was presented to me as a natural progression – an automatic next step in my treatment, rather than something I could actively choose, or refuse, to do. The whole emphasis now would be on rehabilitation and on figuring out, with the help of specialised staff, what level of independence I might be able to achieve and how I could go about attaining this. Perhaps implicit in all of this, and in the move from a purely medical to a rehab ward, was the idea that I'd already more or less completed as much neurological recovery as would be possible and that it was now a case of coming to terms with and learning to live with the limitations of that recovery. However, I wasn't about to just meekly accept the status quo of the degree of improvement I'd achieved by this point.

Conveniently, the BIRU was just a short trolley dash from the neurology ward. On the day I was moved, I felt my mood lift a little at the idea that the transition was something positive, or at the very least something different. I didn't know what to expect, but I did hope that it heralded the end, at last, of the cold and gloom and relentless nightly obs routines of neurology.

Life at the BIRU was certainly different in some important ways. For a start, each patient had their own room with an en suite bathroom and a door that could be closed at night – in itself, a luxury after the ward. Each of us was assigned our own carer, who'd liaise with us daily about a tailored programme of physical rehab. We also worked with occupational therapists to relearn some of the basic skills we'd need to live as independently as possible. In my case, I particularly needed to get accustomed to using my right hand.

What strikes me now about this period is just how relentlessly demanding of myself I was. I had very little capacity for self-compassion or self-care and was uncomfortable when others tried to offer me emotional support. Only rarely did I let up the internal pressure. Even when I ached to just sleep for a decent stretch during the day, I wouldn't allow myself, believing I had to stay active, even if only mentally, for as long as possible. I felt compelled to stick to the small daily routines I'd carved out, believing that letting up would mean that I was in danger of becoming complacent – and complacency would mean that my progress, and any further recovery, would be stalled.

In the same way, I was hypervigilant about what I ate, convinced that if I wasn't, I'd end up being fat as well as lazy. I abjectly refused to eat the hospital food and asked family and friends to bring in what I regarded as healthy alternatives, which mainly consisted of vegetables and fruit. I even took to eating raw broccoli! I can see now that indulging occasionally in the homely hospital food wouldn't have done me any harm and might have provided my body with the comfort that only carbs can bring, as well as some much-needed ballast to help build up my physical strength. I realise, too, that my strict regime of mainly broccoli and soup wouldn't have contained nearly enough of the healthy fats, protein and essential oils my recovering body, and especially my brain, would have been crying out for.

My rigorous self-discipline extended to many other things too. On one occasion, for example, I adamantly refused to let my carer help me shower. 'How will you manage, Rachel?' she protested, but I wasn't listening.

It took me over an hour to have that shower and, as she had predicted, I dropped the soap more than once, but it wasn't really the shower that was the biggest problem; getting myself dressed took another hour. Trying to put my bra on was a phenomenal challenge. It took all my ingenuity and strength, but eventually I managed it. I can only imagine the carer's frustration as she listened to me curse when I lost control and had to start over. But I did it, and it encouraged me to believe that anything is possible. I figured that the rest would be easy in comparison and, from that day on, I did everything for myself.

Perhaps this in itself could be seen as an important step in my recovery – a sign that I'd got some of my mettle back. I can recognise elements of my upbringing, and of my father, in the punishing standards I set for myself and in my almost obsessive conviction that if I didn't keep driving myself, I would be branded lazy and complacent. At this particular juncture, however, my refusal to back down, give up or accept my own limitations was perhaps the main reason I made the progress I ultimately did – progress that, in the years to come, those who cared for me during those dark days at the BIRU would struggle to believe was possible.

As it happened, because it was only my brain's motor centre that had been damaged, I was one of the few BIRU patients at that time whose cognitive abilities hadn't been significantly impaired by my brain injury. The flip side of this was that, physically, I was far more affected than some of the others. Now that she had recovered from her surgery, for example, my old friend Pippa was completely able-bodied. She'd suffered significant damage to some key neurological functions, however, including her short- and long-term memory. Some of the consequences of this were heart-breaking to witness, particularly her inability to recognise her husband or two young children on their frequent visits.

After once again witnessing how her expression hadn't changed to one of recognition as he sat down beside her, I decided to offer some help. Later that day, I broached the matter.

'Pippa, I was just thinking . . . Why don't we agree on some kind of sign I could give you when your husband comes so that you'll know it's him without him having to introduce himself again? I don't know . . . Maybe I could give you a thumbs up, or nod my head towards him or something like that?'

Pippa was pleased with my suggestion. More than anything, she hated seeing the look of hurt and disappointment on her husband's face each time she looked at him as if he were a complete stranger. She said she'd love me to do something. So I agreed to help her in this way, and also to give her quick briefing sessions just before her family were due to visit, to help her recognise them when they arrived.

All of this began to work well and, one day, when Pippa was wondering what she could do for me in return, I suggested that she could sometimes wheel me to the outside area near the unit so that I could get a breath of fresh air and also, I have to confess, have a sneaky cigarette.

The peculiar camaraderie of very sick hospital patients is a dynamic all its own. Perhaps it's the circumstances of your being there in the first place; illness, treatment and death have a strange way of bringing people together. It can, quite literally, feel like a life-or-death situation much of the time, so you have each other's backs in a way that, perhaps, only soldiers or those who work in war or disaster zones might understand. That's the only way I can explain it.

So yes, while smoking wasn't the best thing for me to be doing, it was a valuable opportunity to bond with other patients who were smokers, as well as get respite and mental space from the unit, helping to break up long, boring days of unremitting routine. And the chit-chat provided huge relief. Naturally, the staff, especially our carers, didn't approve, but perhaps because it was one of the few opportunities patients had to assert their individual identities, the staff felt it was better to let the smoking go, as it added to the quality of our everyday lives in a very real way.

It wasn't long before myself and Pippa, the girl who'd once vowed to kill me, became a double act of sorts. Like many relationships that develop at times of crisis, ours was symbiotic, with each providing the other with the things she was lacking. It developed tentatively, as over time each of us sussed out the needs of the other and tried in some way to meet them. Pippa could take on physical tasks for me and I could be her memory so that, together, we made up one fully functional human being. She would wheel me around and sometimes fetch me cigarettes and other things from the nearby garage shop; I would help her to recognise her family – 'Apparently, that's my husband . . .' – as well as provide funny insights into goings-on in the ward. She and I were such different people in terms of personality, background and interests but, somehow, as fellow survivors, we formed a very strong connection, one that really was mutually beneficial.

◆ ◆ ◆

By now my insistence on pushing myself and my determination to make ground in my recovery had become my trademarks. The staff recognised this, and I was gratified when one day one of the occupational therapists approached me to ask if I'd have a chat with a fellow patient. Sophie, who was in her early twenties, had been shot in the head during a drive-by shooting outside a nightclub. As a result, like me, she'd sustained substantial damage to parts of the motor centre in her brain, which had left her struggling with physical coordination, so even the most basic everyday task was hugely challenging.

'Sophie is having a really hard time, Rachel,' the therapist explained. 'She says it's not worth bothering any more with physical therapy or our work with her and is just sitting in her room for hours at a time. She won't even come out to eat her meals in the café.'

I had been aware of the struggles Sophie was having. On a couple of occasions at least, I'd been in the kitchen when she was there, being coached on how to pick up her cup of coffee. After several tries, when her arm kept swooping through the air and crashing down on the countertop, always missing the cup, she'd become very upset and angry and refuse to give it another go. The few times our paths had crossed in the day room more recently, I'd noticed how despondent and withdrawn she was becoming.

So, when I was asked to have a chat with her, as a fellow patient, I was happy to help, and I went on to become a mentor of sorts for Sophie during our shared time in the BIRU. I was able to convince her of the key importance of challenging what her inner voice was telling her as she tried to make herself do things that initially seemed impossible. So, instead of repeatedly saying to herself, 'I can't', when faced with a task, she could instead create an opportunity for progress by saying something like, 'I'm going to give this a try and see what happens.' I seemed instinctively to have worked out for myself the value of positive self-talk and the influence that the internal environment we create has on our thought patterns. I was also discovering a tremendous drive to help and encourage others. I'd been aware of this at other times in my life, most notably in my determination to help Dominic throughout his illness, and now it seemed to have come to the fore once again.

I was soon asked to help other patients in the unit and in doing so found some small sense of purpose and direction, which also drove my own recovery. I realised that if I was telling other people how crucial it was to keep trying and to keep encouraging themselves, I needed to do the same in my own rehab. (This determination to not only 'talk the talk' would eventually enable me to 'walk the walk' as well!) Being a mentor gave me back some pride, and when I wasn't working on my own physical recovery I was quite happy to offer motivation to others. I wasn't all that well myself and still very vulnerable, but I really did want to help others. All of this gave me a much-needed sense of belonging as I continued to make valuable connections with those in the same predicament as me. Perhaps my own suffering had some purpose after all.

Lauraine and I were stationed in one of my favourite spots at the hospital – the smokers' shelter. Just the two of us were there. I was in my wheelchair, wearing my beloved cowboy boots, while Lauraine sat close to me on the makeshift bench for resident smokers. I thought I could sense the very beginnings of spring in the air: a softening in the mid-afternoon light, the first signs of tiny buds on the otherwise bare trees which flanked the patch of grass in front of the shelter. I felt as if I had been in the BIRU for months, and yet it had only been a matter of weeks.

I loved Lauraine's visits. Somehow, she and I always managed some humour, no matter what the circumstances; and the darker, the better, just like with Breeda. There was plenty of fodder for us during my time in the Frenchay. And then there were the opportunities that smoking afforded for people-watching – another of our favourite activities.

'Okay, Rach, I guess we'd better get you back in there again, otherwise they'll be sending out the cavalry,' Lauraine sighed. 'After all, it must be nearly your dinner time by now.' It was only 3.30 p.m., but Lauraine and I loved to mock the hospital meal-time routine, with its ridiculously early times for breakfast, lunch and dinner and the very short intervals in between – more in keeping with an old folks' home.

'Right – but let's just have one more and then we'll go in.'

Lauraine nodded and obligingly lit another cigarette for me, placing it carefully in my right hand. As soon as I took the first drag, something very strange happened. My left hand began to curl ever so slowly.

'Oh my God!' I gasped. 'This is so bizarre . . .'

It was the first time anything like this had happened with my arm since my surgery all those weeks ago.

'Wait – let's see if you can do that again, Rachel . . . It seemed to happen when you took that drag of your cigarette!'

'Ah, I doubt it means anything, Lauraine. It's probably like that time my big toe moved, just some kind of weird muscle spasm or something.' Yet, as I raised the cigarette to my mouth again with my right hand and inhaled deeply, exactly the same thing happened: my left hand curled, and Lauraine and I were so nonplussed that we both burst out into astonished laughter.

'Do it *again*, Rach!'

And when I did, the same thing happened. We couldn't believe it and, for the first time in a very long time, I felt a little flare of excitement. We'd have to tell someone in the unit as soon as we got back!

'It's clearly the nicotine that's doing it, Rachel. Who would have thought? Smoking's good for you after all! Hey, we've made a

120

big discovery here for the world of medicine – have a couple of cig-arettes and you'll be cured of your paralysis. It's a medical miracle!'

◆ ◆ ◆

The incident with my toe that happened on the ward turned out to be neither a fluke nor a false alarm. It began to happen regularly and was a real sign that at last, gradually, some movement was returning.

But my recovery was far from an easy journey – and nowhere near over yet, of course. From the beginning, I'd been absolutely determined that, somehow, I would walk again. My resolve was truly cemented on my first trip out of the BIRU, about a week or so after my arrival, when my carer wheeled me the short distance to a nearby garage and supermarket. After weeks confined to quarters, I'd been looking forward to this glimpse of the world outside.

As we proceeded along the pavement, it was hard to ignore the surreptitious looks of passers-by. No one actually looked at me, let alone made eye contact or greeted me directly. Instead, after a quick, sympathetic acknowledgement of my carer, they would adopt a middle-distance smile and hurry past. I was taken aback; in the little universe of the BIRU, no one seemed in the least fazed by me or my wheelchair. And then it came to me: now I was a *disabled* person and a source of discomfort to other, 'normal' people.

When we got into the shop, the limits of my new reality hit home further. As we reached the till, I had my purse ready. But of course I couldn't see over the counter to the cashier and, naturally, he couldn't see me either, without craning his neck forward. That's when I felt that I really didn't exist in the regular world any more. Instead of making the effort to look over the counter and talk to me directly, the cashier just addressed everything to my carer, who tried to involve me in the process but gave up when the few people waiting in line behind us began very obviously to shift around impatiently. I was left in my own little dimension, completely ignored by everyone.

So this was what it was like to be in a wheelchair all the time; to be a person with 'special needs'. It really didn't feel very special at all. It was then that I made a vow to myself that I would simply not allow myself to be confined to a wheelchair for the rest of my life. I hated the loss of control, and of what I felt was my identity; I hated the thought that others would look at me and pity me and think that my life was boring and unimaginably dull. I realise now of course that this didn't indicate a great deal of maturity on my part, or much of an ability to look beyond the surface of things, but I was only in my mid-thirties at the time. I'd lived an active, very eventful life and couldn't bear the idea that all of this had now been cut short, leaving the vibrant person I had been eternally sidelined.

More determined than ever now, I took the unrelenting work ethic my father had drilled into us from my earliest childhood and applied it to my new situation and the challenge of physical rehab. I was driven. Every day there were sessions in the gym and pool, which started at 9 a.m. and could continue until 4 p.m., depending on the abilities and physical stamina of the patient. I was always ready, champing at the bit first thing in the morning, and I'd be the last patient to leave at 4 p.m. if allowed. I never had to be coaxed; it was more likely that I'd be the one pleading to do another session or trying to persuade the physios to stay on a little longer. Absurdly, I wore my cowboy boots in the gym, not actually because I was so attached to them (although I was), but simply because I had no other footwear; for some reason, I always forgot to ask someone to pick me up a pair of trainers the next time they went shopping.

I can now see that I'd become obsessive about rehab. I would get angry that the sessions were held only on weekdays. I knew that the staff needed time off, yet to me this weekend inactivity seemed a ferocious waste of valuable time. I'd been doing my research and now knew that those who have suffered a brain injury, particularly the kind which causes paralysis, have only a limited window to maximise their potential for recovery. I'd already been able to achieve a degree of recovery some had thought impossible, but I was convinced I was capable of more. And so, even at weekends, I tried to keep occupied and, if possible, to keep moving, whether by doing exercises the physios had recommended or staring at my body, willing it to heal, in an effort to get back more mobility in my left leg.

Soon afterwards came a pivotal moment in my physical recovery. I was not supposed to do anything without assistance, as I was considered a fall hazard, understandably. However, that day I decided that I would get myself up from my bed and, no matter what it took or how long, somehow I was going to get myself to the end of my bed, across the room and stand upright in the corner.

I managed to heave myself to sitting, using my right arm and 'good' leg (also the right one). This in itself took enormous effort and left me puffing and shaky. After I'd gathered my strength again, I hoisted myself to standing (having locked the wheelchair to keep it stable beside me and using it as a crutch), and then began a slow, hopping shuffle across the few feet into the corner of the room. It was bloody tough and I was a bit nervous but, eventually, I made it. I got myself to the wall in the corner of the room and wedged myself in that position, to look back at how far I'd come. I'll never forget that moment. I surveyed the scene; I felt the power. Here I was, wedged in the corner and supporting myself on my good leg, and I had made it all on my own. Small steps, but to me it was enormous because it spelled freedom. I really felt that I'd triumphed, and of course I knew that if I could do this once, then I could do it again. The real fightback had begun.

Meanwhile, I was equally keen to participate in any activities the occupational therapists were able to offer. One day, two of them decided they would guide me through the cooking of a stir-fry. They'd purchased all the ingredients, and when I came into the purpose-built kitchen everything was sitting out, along with all the utensils I'd need, some of which were specially adapted. They wouldn't step in to help unless it was absolutely essential.

It took me almost four hours to cook that stir-fry. The girls were as good as their word and stood back patiently as they watched me washing, slicing and chopping the ingredients as best I could, using my right hand instead of my left, and retrieving the pieces from all over the counter each time they slid away beneath my hand. But when, finally, the dish was ready to eat, we all agreed that it was one of the best stir-fries any of us had ever had.

In spite of how painfully slow I was at everything, I'd enjoyed that cooking session. But the crash back down to earth wasn't long coming. When I remarked that I was going to be a very hungry woman when I was back in my own house, cooking for myself, one of the OTs looked at me with a serious expression.

'But, Rachel, you do realise it will be a long time before you can live on your own?'

'I know I'll take time to get on my feet again, but I'll be able to live independently at some point, won't I?'

'Ah, no, not really, love. It just wouldn't be safe for you, or for Nicola. You're a serious fall risk, and of course you could still have a seizure at any time. So you'd need to have someone in the house with you at all times, especially at night. What would happen if there was an emergency?'

Once more, I could feel my heart sinking. 'So why are we spending all this time doing stuff like this, then?' I snapped, nodding towards the now empty dinner plates.

'Well, it's just something nice for you to do when you do have more time to yourself . . . To keep you busy, or have an outlet for your creativity, your inner Nigella Lawson, you know?'

The banter continued, but only with a huge effort was I able to hide my intense disappointment, my fear and frustration. Learning to use my right arm had been a huge struggle, especially since it was palsied, the nerves damaged from my surgery. Every physical task required effort on a scale I'd never experienced before. Why, then, was I bothering to work so hard if I was never going to have real independence again? That feeling – of fear that I might never regain my independence, or indeed enjoy independence of any kind – took a long time to shake off that evening and it would come back to haunt me many times in the months and years to come.

It was my surgeon, Richard Nelson, who in fact propelled me on the next step on my journey, although, admittedly, he probably didn't realise this at the time. I'd been making more progress in the BIRU than anyone had expected, and by now had gained movement in my left leg and built up a good deal more physical strength and flexibility generally. I was able to sit up by myself, stay vertical for long periods of the day without any of the nausea or dizziness I'd had initially; I could dress myself, shower (albeit very slowly), drink and feed myself (albeit still very clumsily); and now, I could manage a shuffling walk for up to 200 yards, although again I was very slow and had a pronounced limp. As my surgeon and consultant, Mr Nelson had continued to come and see me in the BIRU on his rounds, although naturally far less frequently than when I'd been under his direct supervision on the neurology ward.

On what would be his final consultation with me as an in-patient, he pronounced himself very pleased with the degree of recovery I'd been able to achieve.

'You've been doing so well, Mrs Gotto. Really well – much more so than I, for one, could ever have anticipated. I know you've been working very hard, and your work has certainly paid off.' He looked at me, smiling. 'So, anyway, I don't think you'll need to see me again for a good while. And that's great news, of course! I'm suggesting that I can now sign you off, Mrs Gotto, although you will need to stay for at least another few months at the BIRU, to continue to gather strength and to keep working with the neuro-physiotherapists.'

By now I wasn't listening. I'd heard the words 'I can now sign you off', and I wasn't about to let them go. As Mr Nelson wound up the consultation and wished me well, a plan was forming in my head. I thanked him sincerely for everything he'd done for me – hard to express in a few words – and promised I'd keep in touch.

The next day, I announced to my carer and some of the other staff that I'd decided to go home to Ireland. I explained that I'd very much taken on board everything Richard Nelson had said, and I'd quickly realised that staying on longer as an in-patient wouldn't really move me any further forward in terms of maximising any independence I could achieve – or, almost as importantly, regaining the confidence that I could cope with minimal help. I didn't get a rapturous response.

'You can't be serious?!' said my carer. 'Rachel, you're nowhere near ready to go home! How on earth will you manage? It's such early days for you. And you're still at risk of having a seizure, even with all the meds. Let me talk about this with the whole team and see what their thoughts are. But I'd be very surprised if their verdict isn't exactly the same as mine.'

Shortly afterwards, the nurse manager came into my room, with a couple of other members of staff in tow. All three made their opinions known in no uncertain terms: that I needed at least another few months in the BIRU before I could think about discharging myself.

But my mind was made up. That very night I phoned my brother Adrian and asked him to book a flight over within the next day or two, so that he could come to collect me and we could fly back to Cork. Adrian, too, was alarmed at this sudden development and sounded very unsure.

'I'm coming home, no matter what anyone says. It's just the right thing for me to do now, and no one is going to persuade me otherwise. If you won't come to get me, I'll ring Jane in Taunton – and if she can't do it, I'm sure I'll find someone. I need to go home.'

Johanna, the boat we blew in on, and my father c. 1966.

Me and Dominic, aged five and six.

The pink building is The Pier House, our childhood home.

Dominic, aged twenty-five.

Nic, 1997.

Me, with baby Nicola.

Me, Nicola and Mum, May 2019.

Autumn 2020.

Sixteen

March 2006

As I came round from a fitful sleep, I saw that my surroundings were at once unexpected and very familiar. I was back at home, in our double bed, in the house Nic and I had shared together. Bright light filtered through the oatmeal curtains. I was aware of it being morning but didn't know the hour. For the first time in many weeks, there was complete silence – no background snatches of conversation between hospital staff, no rattling of tea trolleys or electronic bleeping. All was still.

It was then it dawned on me that I was no longer in the BIRU but back in my own home in West Cork, having flown back from Bristol with Adrian in the late afternoon of the previous day.

Still a little disorientated, I began to sit up, pulling my limp arm on to my lap and holding it there while I steadily took in my surroundings. I was home! I was actually home! Looking around, the shock of seeing familiar things made me momentarily forget who I now was. Just for a minute or two, I imagined that nothing had changed. Then, suddenly, I felt unsure. I was hit by the absence of the reassuring sounds of the ward, which spelt medical safety, physical support and security. What had I done by leaving the BIRU so soon – was I really capable of managing without nursing support just yet? And where *was* everyone? Surely I couldn't be here alone, after so many weeks under constant supervision? As I slowly pushed the sheets back, I saw I was still dressed in the clothes I'd been wearing for the journey home.

I called out, 'Mum . . . Mum! Hello . . . Mum!?'

But everything remained silent. Images from the previous evening came back to me. All the family, including Mum and my brothers, as well as Tim and Lauraine, had gathered to greet me on my return.

'There's a couple of people here to welcome you home, Rachel,' Adrian had forewarned me just as we pulled up to the house.

When they saw me, they all let out a big cheer, and I could tell from the bottles of wine and assortment of snacks that the celebrations were already underway. The rest of the evening had passed in a blur, punctuated by gales of laughter, loud, excited chat and general merriment.

As I sat in bed, I remembered everyone plying themselves with wine and the general volume getting louder and louder as they all became first a little tipsy, and then increasingly inebriated. Meanwhile, although I shared their sense of excitement and relief, as an enforced teetotaller, I could only look on. When being discharged, I'd been warned to abstain from alcohol. With a recent brain injury, and having been prescribed a lot of anti-epilepsy medications, it would not be safe for me to drink. After a time, while everyone else partied, I felt myself becoming more and more tired and worn out. It had been quite a day. The last thing I remembered was someone – my mum, I think, along with Lauraine – helping me into bed. And now this. Had they really all left me on my own on my first night out of hospital and gone home? I could only think that the whole gang must have had a little too much to drink and they'd forgotten that I needed help. I found the thought amusing, even oddly reassuring. And in that moment, a seed was planted. I had been alone all night, and I was fine. The solitude and silence felt beautiful – something like a small return to myself. Taking it all in, I could feel the determination rising within, to win this battle to live freely again, no matter what it took. I was going to regain my physical health, and I would make the journey my life's work. And I would get back on the ocean too.

Then I heard it – Mum's voice, shouting, 'Rachel . . . are you okay?' She had let herself in and was on her way down the corridor towards me.

'Mum! I'm here – in bed!'

She appeared at the bedroom door. 'Oh, thank God you're all right. I've no idea what we were all thinking to go home and leave you for the night. I'm really sorry—'

The cringing look on Mum's face in that moment made me smile. It was one of those 'what have I done?' looks, and I laughed as I told her I was really quite tickled that everyone had just upped and offed without a thought, and on my first night at home too! Not wanting her to feel too bad, I quickly let her know that, actually, being left alone had been a happy accident, and the short interval on my own had given me a much-longed-for breathing space. Everything seemed so new, and I must have repeated two or three times how I was so immensely relived to finally sleep in my own bed again. Together we agreed that being in one's own bed was probably one of life's biggest luxuries. I felt myself relax into the moment and smiled happily at my mum as I watched her gather the bits and pieces of clothing I needed for the day. We two had always got on, and there was a comfortableness between us that morning. I was grateful as my long-suffering mother stood patiently by as I determinedly wrestled my way into one item of clothing after another, only asking for help when I couldn't manage it for myself. And finally, when I was decent again, we meandered our way up the corridor and into the kitchen.

'My God, Mum – look at this place! You guys must have had quite some party.'

The kitchen was chaos. Half-finished bottles of wine, plates of food still on the dining table and worktops and the sink piled with glasses and cutlery. Although I felt a little overwhelmed by the mess, there was also something very gratifying about knowing that everyone else was as pleased and relieved that I was finally out of the Frenchay and ready to move on to the next phase of my recovery, whatever that brought.

After the initial flurry of my return home, I set about trying to establish a workable routine to help me live as independently as possible. Once I settled in a bit, I found I was doing relatively well, maintaining all the progress I'd made in the BIRU and getting plenty of practice at putting my recently reacquired life skills to the test. For a while, stir-fry was my signature dish, and I was eventually able to cut my preparation time from four hours to a much more manageable two! After a short time, Nicola, then aged seven, was able to move back in with me. I was beyond happy to be properly reunited with my daughter after so long and to restore some semblance of a normal life with her. Of course, I still wasn't allowed to drive and had to rely on friends and family to take Nicola to and from school, but at least I could be there for her when she got home in the afternoons, get her settled at night and wake her up in the mornings.

I decided to take on a full-time carer for the daytime, and I was lucky enough to find an amazing lady called Heidi. Heidi was relaxed but very capable, and organised everything around the house. Each day, she'd stay with us until early evening, making sure we had something for dinner, and then she'd leave us until the next morning. Initially, I was a little apprehensive about us being on our own overnight, but I soon felt more confident that we could manage and began to enjoy having at least that little bit of independence from other people.

Nicola loved Heidi, and under her tutelage she became a proficient and enthusiastic knitter. I loved her too, for her great sense of humour and her positivity, but also for the way she was with me – never dwelling on my situation or my health and just treating me exactly as she would anyone else. There was no unnecessary fuss; things just were what they were and she didn't overly question or make a big deal of any of it.

We were all settling into a liveable routine of sorts when, for no reason that could really be pinpointed at the time, I suddenly stopped being well, much to everyone's dismay and my distress. I began to have seizures again, and before long I was having as many as twelve or thirteen a day. Unlike the major seizures I suffered prior to and immediately after my pre-op procedure at the Cromwell – which were classed as 'tonic clonic' or 'grand mal' – these were 'focal aware seizures' or 'partial focal seizures'. 'Focal' or 'partial' means that the irregular electrical activity which causes the seizure happens in only one part of the brain, rather than throughout it; accordingly, abnormal movement or sensation is limited to the part of the body corresponding directly to that area of the brain. The other distinguishing feature of these episodes is that the sufferer doesn't lose consciousness at any point.

Although major ('grand mal') seizures are more traumatic for the brain and their emotional aftermath can be very difficult, the fact that during focal aware incidents you are completely conscious of what is happening to you means that the immediate experience of them can be more distressing for the sufferer. In my case, the seizures would sometimes be prefaced by agonising pain in and around my left eye and down the left-hand side of my face, some-times with vision disturbances in the affected eye. These symptoms could last for up to two to three hours. The pain was so severe and all-consuming that you didn't care whether you were alive or dead. As I learned to recognise this as a prelude to a seizure, I would take it as a cue to get myself lying flat on the floor so that I could better cope with what would happen next.

As the seizure began, I would feel a fizzing, like an electri-cal current, in the middle finger of my left hand, which would then appear to travel up my arm, towards my heart and then my head. I say 'would appear to', since in reality the current was of course originating in my brain and running from there into the left-hand side of my body, as opposed to the other way round. This strange phenomenon – of an electrical charge progressively running up and through the affected part of your body – is known as the 'Jacksonian March' (after John Hughlings Jackson, a nine-teenth-century English neurologist renowned for his research on epilepsy). And for the sufferer, it really does feel like a march, as the sensation feels unstoppable, like an army determined to let nothing or no one hold up its advance. My experience was, as the seizure took hold, that this would give rise to the distressing impression that my left arm and leg were flailing and jerking fran-tically. Bizarrely, though, this impression was false, and family or friends who were there to witness these episodes would assure me afterwards that my limbs had stayed still and inert, despite what it felt like to me.

In my case, the seizures could last for up to three minutes. Although this might not sound like a long time, in reality it felt for ever. At the height of the seizure, all my focus would be drawn to my heart and my head; both would feel as if they were about to explode. And all the while, I'd be convinced I was going to die

– that neither my body nor my brain could possibly withstand this visceral assault.

As the seizure eventually waned, my awareness would be dominated by the desperate pounding of my heart: this time, not because of the electrical current, but because of the huge overload of adrenaline that comes from feeling sheer terror. These episodes left me overcome by confusion and exhaustion, emptied of every vestige of energy and strength. The crushing physical weakness in my left arm and on the left side of my body would persist for many hours. Often, all I could do was give in to the need to sob inconsolably, as some way of expressing my helplessness and aloneness. It is very hard to convey just how impotent you feel when you realise you are utterly at the mercy of aberrant electrical impulses which can take over your brain and body at any time and with very little warning.

I've tried to describe here what a typical partial aware seizure could feel like, but in reality my seizures during this period could play out in many different ways, with any number of variations. For example, there was one occasion when my mum, concerned about my state, was taking me to see the local pharmacist. In the car, I began to have what I'd learn to call a 'mini partial seizure'. During these, I neither lost consciousness nor experienced the 'Jacksonian March'; instead, my left arm would begin to curl up and towards my throat, as if I was trying to strangle myself – and of course, there was nothing I could do to stop it. On this occasion, this continued to happen once we got into the pharmacy, much to my distress, as the other customers tried not to stare at these strange antics. At least with grand mal seizures, since you're unconscious, you're spared the mortification of other people's reactions.

◆　◆　◆

The return of the seizures, albeit of a different type, was devastating in every way. I lost much of the ground I'd gained, which I'd been working hard to consolidate since my return home. The increased medication to control the seizures also meant that my will to keep moving and keep pushing myself dissipated almost completely. Worst of all, however, was the renewed sense of precariousness. Being at the mercy of seizures that could strike at any moment, I could no longer count on my ability to keep myself safe, and the confidence that I could more or less cope with everyday life seemed to desert me. The semblance of a normal life, which I had been working so hard to create, simply crumbled.

As soon as I had that first seizure, I had of course been in touch with my GP as a matter of urgency. His response was to up my anti-seizure medication, and to keep doing so as these episodes became more frequent and intrusive. When this didn't seem to help in terms of reducing the seizures, the GP urged me to go back to my neurologist in London. And so I had to make the trip over to the Cromwell again, accompanied by Adrian. Ken Zilkha was glad to see me again, although not at the circumstances of my visit, of course. Once I'd talked through with him what had been happening, he ordered an array of scans and tests to be fast-tracked. When these came through a day later, he called me in again to discuss the findings. Once more, I found myself gazing at a series of images of my brain on a screen.

'Can you see the darker grey areas here, Rachel, in the right-hand motor centre of your brain – where the AVM was originally located? Well, this now shows the laying down of scar tissue at the site of your surgery. As you know, with any wound, scar tissue begins to form once a certain degree of healing has taken place, and it can be very thickened and uncomfortable in the early stages. The scans show the huge level of trauma your brain has suffered and, consequently, the extensive areas of scar tissue which have been forming. While we don't know exactly what has caused these new seizures, my guess is that this has to do with these areas of thickened tissue.'

Dr Zilkha then explained that for the foreseeable future I would need to stop any form of neuro-physiotherapy, even informally, as these sessions were another possible explanation for the seizures. It was possible that the physical therapy work was too stimulating to the brain. Other than this, the only proactive treatment he could now suggest was to keep adjusting my medication to determine the right dosages and combination to keep my brain sufficiently quiet and put a stop to the seizures.

And so the next period of my life was dominated by this attempt to establish a new drug regimen that would restore some stability to my brain. Under Dr Zilkha's direction, the doses of the drugs I was already on were progressively increased, and various other medications gradually added into the mix. Soon I was taking no fewer than six different anti-seizure drugs in significant doses up to four times a day. He also prescribed a programme of benzodiazepines to reduce agitation, promote sleep and further calm my brain. These included a benzodiazepine called Frisium; even now, the very name makes me shudder. At one stage, I was travelling to London every couple of weeks, accompanied each time by a family member or friend, so that I could check in with Dr Zilkha and they could monitor my progress and the efficacy or otherwise of the drugs.

Eventually, the right combination of drugs was found, and the seizures finally stopped. From this point on, my doctor was reluctant to change anything about this apparently effective combination of meds, because of the risk of the seizures returning. They adopted the 'if it ain't broke, then don't fix it' approach.

And I simply went along with the medics' advice. Initially I was just grateful not to have any more of the terrifying seizures – even though I was once again fully dependent on other people, banned from driving and I all but disappeared into a haze. And at first, too, compared to the horror of the seizures, it didn't seem so bad that, emotionally and cognitively, I felt like I'd had a frontal lobotomy, such was the deadening effect of the drugs on my system.

And then I entered the darkest, most directionless and frightening period of my life.

Seventeen

The Spellbound Years

When I look back now at the years after my surgery, once my medication had been regulated so that I was seizure-free, I can see the extent to which I was living a strange, dream-like existence, although I had little awareness at the time that this was the case. It was only relatively recently, when I discovered the work of the US psychiatrist Peter R. Breggin MD, that I was able to make some sense of what was happening to me. His work finally gave me some clue to the puzzle of my altered state during that time.

In his ground-breaking research into the effects of psychotropic drugs and particularly the impact on the brain of 'poly-drugging' – the combining of these drugs – Breggin identified a phenomenon he would christen 'medication spellbinding' (intoxication anosognosia): a drug-induced mental impairment into which the patient has no insight, often believing instead that they are functioning better than previously (that is, pre-treatment), despite all external evidence to the contrary. The person may display uncharacteristically impulsive and potentially destructive tendencies in their decisions and actions, yet they have no awareness of this or of their deteriorating psychological state and may be reluctant to accept an external, objective view of their situation.

Today I can recognise the clear parallels with this phenomenon in my own experience and the way I was living my life during this time, when every day I was ingesting a significant cocktail of psychotropic drugs, as prescribed of course by my doctors. I am now convinced that medication spellbinding played a huge part in the way I was.

On a certain level, to the outside world, I might have appeared to be functioning. Only a few months after my surgery and return to Ireland, I suddenly decided to put my house up for sale, in spite of my very real need to recover and heal and despite advice from friends and family, who questioned the timing of a move and all it would entail so soon into my recovery process. But I didn't listen. Somehow, I managed it. When the house sold very quickly, I asked my brother Nicky and his wife Jan to let me and Nicola live in their house in Glandore village, since they were planning to be in South Africa that winter anyway. It must have seemed to others that I had everything under control and knew exactly what I was doing and, of course, part of me actually believed this.

I then embarked on a series of dysfunctional relationships with completely unsuitable men. Perhaps it seemed to others that I was just determined to make the most of life in spite of all my health problems, and that I was ready to move on from Nic. But the reality was very different. This search for love was not about having fun or moving on from the past. It was a desperate, compulsive, unstoppable need to have a man in my life again, no matter what it took. I was driven to find another soulmate, as soon as possible, so I regarded each one I met as potentially 'the One'. I wanted lasting love, or nothing. I see now that I wasn't ready to move on from Nic, since I'd never allowed myself the time and space to come to terms with losing him, or indeed properly grieved for Dominic. My self-esteem was at rock bottom; I was emotionally blunted, unable to feel anything, good or bad; I had absolutely no real awareness of myself or of other people. Although, in my drug-induced bubble, I felt that I was doing swimmingly, in reality I was certainly not in a good place to find a new relationship.

So these love affairs were doomed from the outset. There are a few episodes in particular that tell of the lengths I was prepared to go to find someone to love me: a short-lived affair with Philip, a surgeon from the UK who I met while on a single-parents holiday, who turned out, once we'd been seeing each other intermittently for a few months, to be married with four children, and not the lone parent of one child that I had met on holiday in the French Alps; a rather wild and dysfunctional relationship with a much older writer; and my eighteen-month entanglement with Stefano, an Italian living in Trieste. In retrospect, I can see an almost comic dimension to all of these 'romances', as well as inherent sadness at the emptiness inside which drove me to such lengths in my search for love.

The writer was older than me by twenty years and quite well known in his field in Ireland and beyond. We met at a smart dinner party, probably about six months after I'd returned from the Frenchay. Initially he seemed entranced by me, in spite of my difficult circumstances. And I suppose I was flattered by his enthusiastic pursuit of me.

Things moved very quickly between us – far too quickly, as ever – and soon I was caught up in the web of a high-energy, intense affair. Being around the writer felt exciting and glamorous and I was powerless at the compulsion I felt to belong in this man's life. My own life of grief and loss appeared so banal in comparison to the wanton and self-indulgent lifestyle that he led and, of course, I was hungry to forget all about the past. Looking back, if I could have listened to my gut, I would absolutely have walked away in the first moment but, nevertheless, at the time, I was attracted to the decadent and, frankly, dark energy that this man gave out. His house was alive with a constant flood of interesting and bookish people who drank long into the night, holding brilliant conversations about erudite matters, the spirit always gossipy and raucous. Probably, I knew then that I didn't belong, but such was my emotional conditioning, and my vulnerable state, that I simply internalised that this was where life was at, and consequently I strove hard to fit in. My own friendships, up until this point, had always thrived on deep and meaningful personal interactions, but in that time I was lost to my true self. The physical side of our relationship never felt entirely easy and natural, but I was content to overlook this without much questioning. I was in love! The writer's world was a beautiful world, with very little room for the ugly, or time for the broken, and soon my presence, as the person I was then, began to irritate him, and the intense interest he'd had in me began to wane as quickly as it had started. The seemingly caring and altruistic veneer began to crack, and beneath it a rather cruel and narcissistic side began to emerge. Our interactions became fractious and loud, and my insecurity grew. And the more unsure I became, the more I clung to the relationship, like a survivor to a raft. Disagreements were frequently alcohol-fuelled, which lent them a cruel edge, and I was often left weeping. I fought to hold on, and I definitely gave as good as I got, and, to a certain degree, I could understand that my emotional neediness must have been infuriating, but his anger meant that I became increasingly clingy. Over time, though, he began to be elusive, and more difficult and distant with me whenever I was around. Another all too familiar pattern was beginning to play out. As was my wont, I initially ignored what was happening and continued in my myopic pursuit of love, despite all the flagrant signs that were beginning to surface. My stultification continued unbroken until, one night, I began to twig that the long and whispered late-night phone conversations were not just of a friendship nature but were intimate and secret. That, coupled with an angry outburst directed at Nicola, made me recognise that I needed to call time on the relationship. As desperate as I was to be loved, I simply couldn't ignore the toxicity between us any longer. Even I, in my dulled-down state, couldn't continue to pretend. It was clear that we did not share love, the writer and I, and I had yet again brought myself and Nicola into a dysfunctional and toxic relationship. The next day I decided to end our connection. It wasn't an easy decision and, although I still desperately hoped that he would ask me to stay, I knew I had to go on my way if I wasn't going to spiral emotionally even further. I also knew, deep down, that he was hoping I would take the hint and go on my way, and so I did.

I continued to be miserable and broken for a few weeks after the whole sordid affair ended and, for a time, I continued to obsessively text the writer because I still naively harboured hopes that I might rekindle a longing in him similar to the one I felt, now that I was, once again, alone. He never replied and I moped around for a few weeks more, but it wasn't long before I'd dusted myself off and renewed my search for the perfect man. I believe now that this relentless pursuit of emotional crash-and-burn scenarios was all part of my 'spellbound' mindset and much of it had its roots in unresolved and unprocessed issues in my childhood. It's clear to me that the relationships I was attracting at the time were all born out of a deep existential longing to belong to someone or something. I had begun life with an emotional deficit, and in life I had lost so much more, and the feelings of abandonment that I harboured deep within me were sufficient to mean that I was willing to engage with, and put up with, almost anything, or anybody, just so I didn't have to be alone with my thoughts and the whispering voices that muttered that I was, in essence, completely unlovable.

Invitations to dinners and parties during this time were frequent. The people in and around Glandore were very generous and supportive in ways I will never forget. Given my history, as one of the Bendon family, and with the various tragedies that had befallen me, most people knew me, had heard about me, or were keen to get to know me. In the locality, I must have been something of an enigmatic, unusual figure: the widow who lived on her own with her young daughter and who had gone through so much in her life, all before the age of forty.

I enjoyed these social occasions – or at least that's what it looked like from the outside. But there was one reason and one reason alone for my happy, bubbly dinner-party demeanour: alcohol. I started to drink alcohol again very soon after I began to socialise again. I was aware that it wasn't advisable, given my health issues, but by that point in my life I'd had so much seriousness that I simply wanted to feel young and that I was like everyone else. I craved levity and freedom, and alcohol provided just that feeling, and so, against better judgement, I began to drink wine when I went out. Once I'd had a few drinks, somehow I really did feel better, or at least more like the person I was before surgery. I seemed to be able to drink copious amounts without ever getting inebriated. It was only years later that I worked out why. Put simply, alcohol had the same effect as topping up my benzo medication (Frisium), giving me the short-lived experience of feeling relatively normal, until the alcohol level fell again and I was once more dropped into what is called tolerance withdrawal. I had become tolerant to the drug and it was no longer doing its job of keeping me calm and relaxed; quite the opposite. Seven years on a stable dose of Frisium meant I'd become physically dependent on it (very different to psychological dependence), causing me to feel depressed and withdrawn. I was in tolerance withdrawal for years, and the only way to alleviate this would be to take more of the drug or to successfully withdraw. It's a complex area and I knew nothing at all about it at the time, and neither, so it seems, did my doctors. So I continued to take Frisium daily for years and my suffering was only alleviated when I drank. No matter how much I consumed, I could never get drunk, but the side effect was that the alcohol lifted me out of this awful flat world of depression, anxiety and insomnia. No wonder, then, that I began to rely on it to be able to socialise. It makes me sick now to think back to how much I could drink, and did, and the fact that I managed somehow to stay alive, because there is a direct link between benzodiazepine consumption and alcohol abuse causing respiratory failure. Where would Nicola have been then?

But while in social settings I seemed to be having fun, the reality of my daily existence was very different. In truth, I was a mere shell, with no substance and no inner life to speak of. My days were a blur of grey exhaustion. Every morning, I'd have to fight the urge to keep sleeping and get up to make sure Nicola left for school, then I'd return to my bed for the rest of the day, setting my alarm clock for late afternoon so that I'd be more or less awake again for Nicola coming home. After that, I'd drag myself through the evening hours, somehow summoning the strength to throw together a couple of basic ingredients for dinner (we probably ate more or less the same thing every night during that time). Once that was done, I'd patiently wait until Nicola's bedtime so I too could get to bed.

Every night, while she slept, I'd be consumed with dread at the prospect of the hours that stretched ahead, for I could never sleep or get any kind of respite or relaxation. Lying in the dark, I was at the mercy of my restless body and even more restive mind. And all the while, I kept ingesting the regular top-ups of the mind-numbing meds I now expected to be on for the rest of my life. In all the most telling ways, I was living like a drug addict, merely eking out the hours until the next fix. Only on Saturday nights, when my mum had Nicola to stay over, could I expect a little levity, as I'd get to go out with a girlfriend or to a dinner party and find some relief in alcohol.

After the affair with the writer, I'd turned to internet dating in my relentless determination to find love. Somehow, it seemed to be perfectly suited to my lifestyle of being a single mum at home and unable to do anything very active or physically and mentally demanding. I was so isolated and alone, and the 24/7 nature of the online world seemed to help.

◆ ◆ ◆

Before long, I had hooked up online with the Italian guy, Stefano. Once again, things developed very rapidly, and soon we were in constant contact. Just a few short weeks into our relationship, he came to visit me for a weekend in The Farm House, where Nicola and I had moved after the relationship with the writer. By the time the weekend was drawing to a close, I had booked flights to see him within the month. After a couple of weekends together, I decided that this time I really had found the right guy and excitedly told my friends and family all about him.

We quickly settled into a regular pattern of spending alternate weekends in West Cork and Trieste, and this continued for the next year or so. Completely caught up with the distraction of a new and different relationship, I managed to convince myself that this was love, although, looking back, deep down, I felt very little for him. Stefano was very handsome, and of course the fact he was Italian lent an extra edge of glamour to him and to our romance, as did the long-distance aspect of the relationship. He and Nicola also seemed to get on very well together. He seemed happy to go on bike rides and watch *The Simpsons* with her. To me, he genuinely seemed to enjoy all of this. In hindsight, it's clear that this was because my new boyfriend was still very much a child himself!

Soon what was on offer wasn't enough for me. I craved the commitment of being together 24/7 and the knowledge that every part of my life was inextricably bound up with that of the man I was with. I was desperately trying to recreate what I'd had with Nic and fill the huge void left when he died. And so, hard as it is to believe now, after less than a year together I took it into my head that for the relationship to really work, Nicola and I would have to move to Italy to be with a man I didn't actually know that much about, given the distance factor, the language gap (especially initially, I didn't speak much Italian, although he spoke very good English) and the fact that our weekends together were spent in a haze of romance, newness and cultural exploration.

When I told friends and family of my plans, they were, frankly, worried sick. I'd only known this guy for a relatively short time – certainly not long enough to get a real sense of who he was and of whether we had anything in common. I'd never seen him in everyday, run-of-the-mill circumstances. Was I really going to uproot my daughter, rent out my house and put myself in such a vulnerable, risky situation when I was still so physically and psychologically under par? Thinking about it now, I'm appalled at how, once more, I just bulldozed my way through other people's concerns. Not for a moment did I give any serious consideration to what those who cared about me were saying. I knew what I wanted to do, and no one was going to stop me. That it had been just a few years since I'd had life-changing brain surgery was irrelevant.

Today I can recognise this as just one more illustration of the extent to which I was 'spellbound' at that time. The impetuousness, the recklessness, with which I approached both my own life and that of my young daughter, whom I loved more than anything, did not at all represent the person I really was, or am. Although I'd always been strong-willed, I'd always been good at thinking things through, and at least teasing out the pros and cons of important situations before acting. This kind of poor impulse control, and complete, unwavering (and illusory) belief in my own invulnerability, is typical of the self-destructive traits that Dr Peter Breggin has identified in those who have poorly tolerated the increasingly common practice of poly-drugging with benzodiazepines and other psychiatric medications.

And so, in the summer of 2010, Nicola and I transplanted our lives to Trieste. Neither of us spoke Italian, although, before we left, I did arrange for us each to have sessions with a private tutor so that we could pick up a few basics. I certainly had no experience of living abroad. I enrolled Nicola in an international school, rented a house nearby, and Stefano left his little flat at his parents' house and moved in with us. Once again, I had silenced my critics, and since I was financially independent, there was really nothing to stop me moving to be with a man I was certain was the new love of my life.

The truth was that, while I thought myself to be madly in love with Stefano, once we were together full-time, I soon realised that I actually didn't like him very much. Yes, he was physically attractive, and although he wasn't my usual type, his height and bearded good looks interested me and he could be extremely charismatic, but he was also self-involved, had no real substance and was prone to tantrums and prolonged periods of silent sulking if he didn't get his own way. Our relationship was all drama, with lots of passionate arguing and slamming of doors – things which at the time I told myself were typical (and exciting) features of grand passion, but which were exhausting and toxic to live with on a daily basis. Perhaps part of the reason I was attracted to Stefano was because, being so demonstrative and vocal about his emotions, he was very different to a lot of men I'd been out with – and at first, I enjoyed the novelty. But there was little tenderness, caring or consideration between us, and when it came to the arguments and unpleasantness, I always gave as good as I got.

It wasn't long before the relationship began to play out in the same way as it had with the writer. Unable to cope with my intensity, he began to tire of me. Meanwhile, he began to bore me, and his tantrums frightened me. After just three months or so, I had moved into the spare room to sleep near Nicola, while Stefano seemed quite happy to have the main bedroom, even though this was effectively my house, as I paid most of the rent and the lease was in my name.

As things became more and more untenable, I suggested that he move out for a time with a view to working on the relationship, although, privately, I had no intention of doing so; it just felt like a safer way to put distance between us. He reluctantly accepted. Then, one day, he asked if he was in my will. This shocked me and made me feel very insecure. Although I refused to see it at the time, it was clear that, in emotional terms, he was nothing more than an overgrown child. Perhaps that's why he enjoyed spending so much time riding his scooter with my ten-year-old daughter! And when, after he moved out, his elderly aunt appeared on my doorstep several times to try and get me to take him back, it was impossible to ignore the fact any longer that he was woefully immature and still tied to his beloved auntie's apron strings.

Even though the relationship was in its final throes, it didn't feel right to uproot Nicola once again and simply go back home to Ireland. We had made some nice friends in Trieste, in particular a Danish family with two kids in the same age bracket as Nicola. Although life for Nicola was not that easy, given the mother I was then, to this day she tells me she's glad we spent that time in Italy, in spite of what later transpired. I also felt deeply ashamed of the fact that it hadn't worked out with Stefano and couldn't bear the idea of returning to Glandore, where all our friends and family would know of yet another love failure. It's clear to me now that they certainly wouldn't have been smug if we had gone back, but at the time my own inner critic was very harsh and unforgiving and I was convinced that other people's judgements of me would also be harsh and certainly more than I was able to handle.

So, we stayed on in Trieste for two years, even though Stefano was no longer a part of our lives. As weeks turned into months, however, and now that I no longer had the drama of a volatile love affair to distract me, I began to realise that I wasn't doing very well at all. The truth was that I was living the same kind of twilight existence as I had in Glandore. My days were spent sleeping because of the most awful intractable insomnia that plagued my nights, punctuated only by the necessity of getting Nicola to school and to at least be awake by the time she came back. Nights were sleepless. Unable to stay still, I would pace the room to stave off the ever-present anxiety, and then, as the sun rose, along with it came the desperation that comes when sleep continues to elude you. As before in Ireland, the only times I felt halfway human were when I was drinking. I never drank alone, even then, so if I was invited to friends' houses at weekends, I'd leap at the opportunity. It was a miserable, soulless existence, but because I was so bombed by the drugs, so spellbound, I wasn't even able to recognise it as such.

It was Nicola who forced me finally to acknowledge that neither of us was coping with life in Trieste. When we'd initially arrived in Italy, Nicola adjusted remarkably well and had quickly taken to life in another country. She'd also settled in to the set-up at the international school and seemed to enjoy it all, finding that in some ways she had more in common with her classmates there than in Glandore – although when it came to socialising with her peers outside school, language could be a barrier, as everyone spoke Italian when not in class.

Shortly after my break-up with Stefano, Nicola began to become fretful and uneasy. Soon she was having full-blown panic attacks when leaving me, as well as periods of intense anxiety in between attacks. She lost confidence and was finding it difficult to sleep unless I held her hand. Lessons at the international school had become very demanding now that she was older, with students expected to spend long hours on homework. Things had shifted into a much faster, more competitive gear, and the pressure was too much. But this wasn't the only thing causing Nicola to struggle. It was clear that all the traumas and bad patches we had weathered were beginning to catch up with my daughter. She had grown up without meeting her father; she'd had serious health problems herself during the early months of her life; she had witnessed me going through the dramatic and painful stages of my AVM diagnosis and recovery from life-or-death brain surgery. Over and above all this, she'd lived most of her life with a mother who was simply not physically able to be as present for her as she should have been, and who had very little mental and emotional energy to spare.

With the panic attacks, Nicola began to be afraid even to go into school. Deeply concerned, I did everything I could to help. I removed her from school. At night, I'd sit at her bedside, holding her hand until she finally fell asleep. Often, I'd stay all night, knowing that, in any case, I'd be unable to sleep myself if I went back to my own room. I hired a private tutor, Michael, who came to the house to give Nicola her lessons: this seemed to help considerably, allowing her to find some distraction in whatever subject they were working on. She got along well with Michael, which was in itself therapeutic. But I knew it was far from ideal, and certainly not a solution in the long term.

The extent to which Nicola was suffering forced me to stop and seriously take stock of our situation. I told her I would be willing and indeed happy to move back to Ireland straight away, if she felt that would help her and make her feel any better. Initially, she insisted that Italy wasn't the problem at all – that, actually, she was glad we'd moved as it had given her the opportunity to experience a world beyond West Cork. And for a while I took her at her word. But more and more often, I'd find myself in tears when talking to Mum, until I finally admitted to her that, on top of my own physical and mental state, I was beset with anxieties about Nicola, and that both of us were really struggling in Italy. As always, Mum listened and allowed me to talk everything through without judging or saying 'I told you so.' For a few months I went back and forward in my mind about what I should do, until eventually I admitted to myself and then to Mum that the best thing for Nicola, and for me, would be to return to West Cork. Only years later, when Nicola was twenty, did she tell me that her anxiety around school was because she feared that I would just up and leave her one day, that she would come home and find me gone and she would be all alone in Italy. My heart still breaks at this; my poor, poor girl.

Eighteen

July 2010

I'm in a waking nightmare. A tiny black beetle is running up and down my forearm. I can't quite take it in. Something within me is repulsed. I try to sweep the beetle off my arm and away from my body, but it's no good. Nothing I do makes any difference.

Horrified, I crash my way into the cool darkness of the bathroom, where I flick on the light and stand staring at myself in the mirror. Turning on the cold tap, I frantically sluice water on to my face in the hope that the shock will dispel the awfulness and that I'll awaken to find it's all been a terrifying dream. The beetle is no longer on my arm, but as I straighten up I see my reflection in the mirror again. My face doesn't belong to me. I look somehow altered. I'm panicking now, my heart pounding. Worse than this, I see a mass of squirming black pin-like worms crawling out of my mouth. Earlier in the day, I'd held a hedgehog whose body had been invaded by hordes of worms. Now what feels like hundreds of them are wriggling and pushing against my tongue. I drop to my hands and knees, transfixed with horror. What's happening? The panic no longer comes in waves. I am drowning in it. If this is real, what is this evil new world?

If this is dying, it's not as I imagined. It's not the benign, peaceful surrender to the natural order of things; it's not the experience of inscrutable beauty I glimpsed as I sat with Dominic in his final weeks. If this, now, is death, it's total isolation, the certainty that there is no escape.

As I sit there for God knows how long, I try to force myself to focus on what lies in my immediate line of sight. Perhaps the sight of familiar objects will stop the horror in its tracks – or at least make it recede. I see the bathroom scales upright against the wall opposite me, the toilet brush in its holder, tucked in beside the toilet. I see the bathmat on the floor. But none of these objects is familiar or reassuring now; they are bizarre, meaningless artefacts which loom towards me, menacingly.

Suddenly I feel the hatred of the whole world directed at me. It's as if every single negative experience I've ever had has been magnified. I hear my father's derision. I feel deep shame, and, wholly wrong, rotten to my core, that everyone sees me for who I am. All my worst fears about myself are vying with each other to be heard. My mind is racing. Evil is in here and it's punishing me.

Then the voices begin. They are judging me, shouting over one another to tell me what they think. I don't know if this cacophony of evil, this relentless chanting and wailing, is real or in my head, contained within the narrow confines of my flesh-and-blood skull.

'Don't you know how much we hate you, Rachel? You're pathetic; you always have been. We hate you, and they all hate you too. Dominic and Nic hated you. That's why they both left you, don't you see? It's what your dad always tried to tell you – at least he was honest about it. The others have only ever been pretending. Everything about you is repellent. You make us sick!'

And on and on and on it goes – an endless stream of vitriol and loathing. I clamp my hands to the side of my head and shout: 'For Christ's sake, STOP!'

Some time later, after what feels like hours, I heave myself up off the floor, my legs weak and trembling. The torrent of adrenaline has left my whole body limp and feeble. With my hands still pressed desperately to either side of my skull, I slowly make my way into the kitchen, stumbling as I go.

I feel almost at the end of everything, that this will be my one last effort to save myself. It's the same feeling I had after the catastrophic seizures I suffered post-surgery, all those years ago. As if I'm at the very base of a very high cliff, trying to make my voice heard by those who exist in the plane above me, a place of connection and love. But my voice is too weak. I'm spent.

Then, in an instant, I know what to do. I grab some Frisium from my bag, pop open one of the little cells and swallow one of the tiny white tablets. Then I curl up into a foetal position and wait. With my demons still breathing down my neck, I wait.

Gradually, the horror recedes. The voices slowly grow silent. I open my eyes and feel some sense of normality returning. The terror which so recently had been thick and choking has at last lifted. I look at both of my arms in turn; there are no beetles. I touch my fingers to my mouth and feel no writhing worms or other awful aberrations. I notice how cold the house is. It is all normal, reassuringly banal. I begin to relax.

In place of horror there now comes bone-crushing fatigue. Everything is stillness as I lie there, whimpering.

Some days earlier, I'd been to see yet another neurologist, hoping for a fresh opinion on how my medication might be contributing to my deteriorating psychological and physical state. Since my return to Ireland, I'd felt that the deadening effect of the drugs I'd been taking was only intensifying. I was eking out a sepia half-life. I couldn't resign myself to decades as a semi-comatose automaton. Nothing had the power to move me any more. I put on a front for other people's sake, particularly for my close loved ones, but that's all it was.

I'd been taken off Dr Ken Zilkha's list some time back; by then he was in his mid-eighties and it was time I had someone more professionally up-to-date to look after my needs. I'd seen a series of consultants in Ireland, but all of them had insisted that the way I was feeling, my diminished quality of life, was a direct result of the brain damage I'd suffered during surgery and that it was highly unlikely that my medication regime was contributing to my difficulties. Each one warned against trying to reduce the doses of any medication, let alone cutting them out altogether: their common mindset was clearly one of 'Don't upset the apple cart.'

But my own instincts were telling me that it was completely possible that the cumulative effect of being on all these drugs for so many years was responsible, at least in part, for the grey blankness of my everyday life. Yet, again and again, I was being told by apparent experts that this just couldn't be the case. None of them seemed to understand, or acknowledge, the basic truth I was trying to convey: that, for me, my life was no longer liveable the way it was; that I was broken, and I was desperately looking for someone willing to try to give some credence to my gut feeling.

Finally, a neurologist reluctantly conceded that one of the drugs I was on – Frisium – could, just conceivably, be magnifying the dulling effects of what he referred to as my 'irreversible brain damage'. He didn't want to go against the recommendations of the team at the Cromwell, all very eminent in their field, but he suggested I try stopping Frisium for a while. 'See how you go,' he said. 'And how do I do that?' I asked. 'Just stop taking it,' he replied.

So, I followed his advice. The next day I simply skipped my morning dose of Frisium (I was still on a four-times-daily dose of all six of my original medications). Nicola would be at school and then staying over with Mum that evening, so I knew I wouldn't have to make dinner for her and get her settled for the night. Not that I was expecting anything dramatic to happen.

Then, just hours later, I found myself plunged into the torment described above. As soon as I took my regular dose again, I almost immediately felt 'normal' once more – or should I say, the disconnected, flat state which had been my normal for so long. No matter how deadening, it was still infinitely preferable.

Later, once I'd recovered to some degree, I set about doing as much research as I could about Frisium. Although apparently it wasn't widely accepted knowledge among expert practitioners at that time, my internet research quickly threw up a plethora of evidence which suggested that this drug, and other benzodiazepines like it, should never be simply stopped outright, without some kind of tapering-off process, particularly in people who have been on the drug for any extended period of time. As I persisted in my online investigations, I also found a lot of information about the work of Professor Heather Ashton, who over a long and distinguished career as a professor of clinical psychopharmacology has pioneered and published some really significant research about the dangers of benzodiazepines. All of her work also pointed to the conclusion that it could be very dangerous – even, in some cases, fatal – to abruptly stop taking these medications.

In the *Ashton Manual* (*Benzodiazepines: How they work and how to withdraw*), which was first published in 2001, Professor Ashton sets out the very compelling case that benzodiazepines create strong physical dependence in the user. The consequence of this is that if the drug is stopped abruptly, for whatever reason, the user will experience withdrawal symptoms that will make them feel mentally and physically very ill; these will disappear again once the drug is resumed at the habitual dose. Long-term use of drugs that cause physical dependence can create changes in the brain, which in turn can lead to mental-health disorders, including addiction.

The difference between physical and psychological dependence may seem inconsequential to some, but it's an important distinction. Psychological dependence, or addiction, is marked by a persistent strong urge to use drugs despite the negative consequences. On the other hand, it's possible to be physically dependent on drugs without being psychologically dependent; for example, someone using prescription drugs under medical supervision, say one of the benzodiazepines used to treat chronic insomnia, can become physically dependent without experiencing compulsive, uncontrollable urges to use. And you can also be psychologically dependent on a substance without being physically dependent; for example, marijuana may not cause physical withdrawal symptoms in everyone, but a user may find themselves unable to quit for psychological reasons.

In any case, everything I read in her manual, and in testimonies of the people Professor Ashton treated in the benzodiazepine withdrawal clinic she ran from 1982 to 1994, confirmed my conclusion that the awful experience I had after suddenly stopping Frisium could be explained by the high degree of physical dependence I'd developed on this drug after such a long period of use.

When I shared these findings with those close to me, they were very concerned. This was a new conundrum. If the drugs were keeping me seizure free and yet, at the same time, making me sick, what to do? I'd told them about the horror of my recent 'cold turkey' experience, so they were understandably very concerned that I would contemplate continuing along this path. I faced mixed opinions and, of course, I and others feared a return of the seizures if I began to change my medications. I was full of doubt. I was also alone in making any decisions, as my recent horrific experience, which had resulted from poor medical advice, meant I'd lost faith in the medical profession to help me navigate this problem.

Why couldn't I just accept where I was at and be thankful for the extent of recovery I had achieved? This question whirled around my mind. I certainly had no wish to have any more 'bad trips', and surely life could be bearable enough if I just knuckled down and acknowledged the fact that I would never be the same person again?

As the weeks passed, I realised that this was something I couldn't do. Quite simply, I couldn't stand myself – the person I was at that time – any longer. I was dragging myself through the days and barely surviving the anguished nights. I felt no sense of connection with anyone, even my closest family and friends. My research meant I'd also become convinced that my zombie-like state had been further deteriorating as time went on and would continue to do so unless something changed. I hated that my short- and long-term memory was shot, that I couldn't even remember what age my daughter was or recall anything very much from her child-hood. I was convinced that these memory problems were becoming more entrenched. And I knew that the incapacitating depression and anxiety were getting worse.

The final straw came the day after Nicola and I had cuddled up to watch the movie *Fifty First Dates* together. Apparently, we'd enjoyed the movie immensely and laughed a lot. I say 'apparently' because, when Nicola remarked the next morning how much fun we'd had and what a great film it was, I'd just stared at her, uncomprehending.

'What movie did we watch, darling? I seem to have forgotten what it was about . . .'

'Mum, we watched *Fifty First Dates* . . . It was brilliant! Don't you remember?'

'Hmmm – no, I don't remember. What was it about?'

'It was about this guy meeting a woman on the beach one day and falling in love with her straight away . . . But then he discovers that she has no memory and that, each day, she's completely forgotten anything that happened the day before. So, every time they meet for another date, for her, it's like they're seeing each other for the first time – she doesn't recognise him and has no memory of what they did the last time. So he decides that he's going to win her over by treating every time they meet like it's their very first date, which, for her, it is, really. Very romantic, actually – but really funny too . . .'

'Nope, darling, sorry, I can't remember any of that.'

The irony of all this was hard to ignore, but at the same time we both saw the humour in it. The woman with no memory who didn't remember watching a film about a woman with no memory. As we so often did, we could laugh at my disability, which saved us from dwelling with any sadness on how limited our connection with each other could be as a result of it.

But later that night, when Nicola had gone to bed, the sadness came, and I couldn't shake it off. I was frustrated at the way things had turned out for us, and at the inescapable awareness of how much my shortcomings and suffering were affecting my daughter. And I felt a deep sense of grief for what we could, and should, have had together. That grief stayed with me for a long while afterwards, until gradually it cemented into an absolute determination that I was not going to accept the way things were any longer. No matter what it took, or how long, I was going to wean myself off those drugs. I needed to know for sure what was brain damage and what was drug damage.

Nineteen

The Dream

It's a beautiful evening in late July. The sun is still high in a cloud-less sky, and the sea is calm, with barely a ripple. Gentle currents of warm air roll in from the Atlantic Ocean. It has been a hot, almost tropical day in the microclimate of this part of the West Cork coastline, but now the heat is much less intense; the sea air is more soothing, yet still rich and salty and holding all the vibrancy of high summer.

Nic is planning to take a group of divers out for a recreational dive, and because it's such a lovely evening he also wants to dive himself, although it wasn't our original plan. His two daughters, Emily and Hayley, are visiting us for the weekend. We'd promised to take them for dinner before dropping them all off at a local disco for teenagers and I was going to stay behind and help them get ready. But the evening is so beautiful that Nic can't resist the idea of a dive so he asks me if I will come along and man the boat while he joins the others. I hum and haw and eventually give in and say that I'll go along, leaving him free to dive. The idea is to dive the wreck of the *Kowloon Bridge*, a massive oil tanker sunk in relatively shallow waters off Castletownshend Harbour. The wreck is only about 35 metres at its deepest point, so easily accessible with traditional scuba equipment. I'm almost six months pregnant by now and reluctantly gave up deep-sea diving months ago, so I'm a great addition to the boat as a non-diver who is experienced with boats.

The only other person in the party, aside from the divers, will be Marie, the wife of Ron, one of the divers, and I'll happily skipper the boat and keep watch once the guys are underwater. This means that all the divers can go in in twos, one couple after another, rather than Nic having to stay behind and look after the boat. That's what we will do this evening. I've always been confident on boats, even more so since I've become involved in Nic's diving business.

As we park our jeep near the quayside, I can see that the other divers are all there already, sorting their gear and readying themselves to get on to the boat. Nic and I clamber aboard; Nic begins to prepare his own gear. Tonight he will not use traditional standard scuba gear and instead opts for his new rebreather. It's a rather curious machine that allows the diver longer bottom time, and with the absence of bubbles. Quite simply, a rebreather recirculates the air breathed in a closed loop and a scrubber removes the carbon dioxide, leaving the diver much more dive time and the added beauty of no bubbles, which is a great advantage when looking at sea life. They are often used for much deeper dives than this, but Nic is still getting familiar with his. It is a closed system and is rather high tech, being governed by two handheld computers attached to the main machine via hoses. So Nic's bright yellow machine stands out from the rest of the kit and, naturally, the others are curious about it. I hear Nic say that he is having difficulty calibrating the machine and that he is not getting the 'safe to dive' mode and then a few minutes later he remarks it 'seems to be okay now'. I don't pay much attention and carry on readying the boat for sea.

'What a gorgeous evening,' I say, and I'm delighted now that I've decided to go out with the gang. I'll get back to Emily and

Hayley later on. I don't think any more about it as we cast off and pull out of the tiny harbour.

As I chat away to some of the guys, my eyes meet Nic's and we exchange smiles. I can sense his excitement at the prospect of the dive and his joy as he inhales the sea air and turns his face fully into the still-hot evening sun. And I know I am happy, happier than I have ever been, with this steady man who has changed my world and soothed my soul. My thoughts shift, as they often do these days, to the baby inside me and I feel a lurch of excitement at the idea of the new adventure we have ahead of us now, in just a few short months' time.

But suddenly this idyllic picture, so vivid in my mind, grows black and disappears. Everything which was bright is now dark, as if the heat and light of the sun has been obscured by a cold, dense shadow. And I'm afraid, I'm so, so afraid. The darkness is all-enveloping, and I cannot breathe. I feel dread, deep in my belly, deep in my core and I know something terrible is just ahead. A wave of panic breaks over me. And then it's black, everything is black . . .

Twenty

October 2010

In the autumn I finally decided that I would begin to wean myself off the prescribed medications I'd been taking since my brain surgery. I would never know what else life might hold for me if I didn't at least try. The first phase of my plan would be to cut down slowly and then completely stop Frisium, which was the only benzodiazepine I was on. After that, I could set about doing the same with the many other drugs I'd been taking since my surgery.

I was convinced of this path of action. All my research seemed to confirm that Frisium was the most dangerous of my drugs in terms of its long-term effects. The second phase would involve weaning myself off as many of the anticonvulsants as possible, very cautiously and gradually. That I'd have to be extremely careful was something I was all too aware of, since the last thing I wanted was a return of the damaging seizures the drugs had been prescribed to prevent. So, this second stage was definitely on the backburner for now, and also depended on how successful I was in getting off the benzodiazepine first.

Through my research, I'd been fortunate enough to discover a fantastic website, Benzo Buddies (www.benzobuddies.org), which offered a wealth of experiential advice and guidance, as well as hosting a well-regulated forum where people with the same goal of coming off benzodiazepines could share experiences and lend support to one another. This site and its associated forum would become an absolute lifeline for me during the long months of my withdrawal. I can honestly say that I don't know if I would still be here today, or have achieved all that I have, if I hadn't had this invaluable 24/7 resource to call upon. I know there is a lot said about the pitfalls and the dark side of the online world but, for me, this is one really compelling example of the positive things the internet has to offer: a source of support, information and reassurance which just would not have existed previously. At a time when I so often felt hopeless and utterly alone, it transformed the quality of my everyday life and kept me engaged and functioning in some shape or form until I'd recovered enough to be able to go out into the world again.

In planning my withdrawal process, I had concluded that the approach advocated by Professor Heather Ashton was the only well-documented and authoritative one. A key method proposed in the *Ashton Manual* is the 'substitution taper', which involves switching from your current benzodiazepine to Valium (another benzodiazepine), especially if the drug you are on has a short half-life – is one that stays in your system for a relatively short time – which means that withdrawal will be felt more quickly and acutely. Since Valium has a particularly long half-life (up to 100 hours), it offers the chance of minimising withdrawal effects as you cut the dose by allowing you to make much smaller reductions at a time. Frisium is a very potent benzodiazepine with a fairly short half-life, so, in my case, the switch to Valium would be an important first step in my withdrawal journey.

Another key part of my preparations was to draw up a provisional 'tapering' schedule for the months ahead, setting out the time frames within which I would be aiming to progressively cut my dose, and by how much at each point. Again, I based my calculations on the *Ashton Manual*'s recommendations; that is, once I had made the switch to Valium, I would be aiming to cut the dose every two weeks by 5 per cent of the total dose, meaning that I'd be reducing it in smaller increments each time, since the total dose itself would be decreasing at each stage. I knew, though, that this could only ever be a tentative schedule, and one that would need to evolve once I'd started the withdrawal process and got a sense of what I could tolerate. Depending on how I was managing, I might have to sometimes allow myself smaller dose reductions or a longer period between tapers.

I'd very much heeded Professor Ashton's advice that withdrawal from benzos is never a 'one-size-fits-all' process, since everyone's body chemistry, state of health and circumstances are different, as is the severity of withdrawal side effects experienced by each person. Another crucial consideration is the length of time someone has been on them; the longer the time, the more difficult withdrawal will probably be. In a case like mine, where I'd been on Frisium for eight years, it was clear that my body's dependence on it would be deeply entrenched and that I could expect a rocky road ahead. Nothing had demonstrated that more starkly than the horrific experience I'd had so recently when I'd tried to stop Frisium outright.

The guidance offered in the *Ashton Manual* covers more than just clinical recommendations about medications and dosages, however. Other equally important aspects are addressed, such as how to put in place some basic emotional and physical support frameworks before embarking on the withdrawal process. Ideally, these should include a range of people who are able to provide encouragement and guidance of both a professional and personal kind. For this reason, I decided that I'd enlist the help of several complementary healthcare professionals. Some were people I'd been maintaining regular contact with since I'd returned to Ireland from the Frenchay, who'd helped me at various points with the ongoing physical challenges I'd been left with in the aftermath of surgery. I decided that I would step up my work with some of them as I embarked on this new challenge. Others I'd be working with for the first time, in the hope that their particular expertise would help make withdrawal a little easier.

There was Dr Stephen Gascoigne, a medical doctor, acupuncturist and Chinese herbalist, who had a very successful clinic in West Cork, with whom I'd been having acupuncture sessions off and on since my discharge from the BIRU. I'd found acupuncture really helpful for many of my post-surgery physical problems. While in hospital and later in the BIRU, I'd also had daily sessions with an amazing acupuncture specialist there, Henry McGrath, which had really aided my recovery. Now I got in touch with Stephen Gascoigne again, telling him what I was proposing and asking if we could set up our appointments during the period ahead where I'd be switching from Frisium to Valium, and then as I aimed to gradually cut out Valium altogether. As a medical doctor, and one who had often questioned the value of some conventional pharmaceutical treatments, Stephen had a really good understanding of what I was facing and was immediately supportive, saying that he would help me as much as he could. Alongside his clinical expertise, he has always had the most non-judgemental, calm and compassionate approach.

Another alternative health professional I'd already been seeing for some time was Florence Vion, a French osteopath based in Clonakilty. Florence's work on easing out and stretching my muscles over the years had really helped with the painful tightness of muscles that have been spastic, which I'd suffered from since the surgery. Again, I told her about my plan, and together we agreed to increase the frequency of our sessions once I started the process. Florence confirmed what I'd already suspected and feared – that, since Frisium is a muscle relaxant, as I began to come off it I would very likely experience more frequent and intense problems with muscle pain and spasming than before, as my body adjusted to no longer relying on a synthetic agent to manage the tension. Like Stephen, Florence would prove to be an invaluable ally in the months to come.

I frequently attended a wonderful homeopath, Bernie Smyth, who worked tirelessly to try to keep me emotionally stable. Her willingness to listen and her accepting and calm approach were often the only things that got me through yet another day of relentless suffering.

Much later down the line, at Florence's suggestion, I began working with a local yoga teacher, Jessica Hatchett, with whom I took one-to-one remedial yoga classes.

As I began this process, I became severely agoraphobic, and for quite some time was unable to step outside my front door without suffering disabling panic attacks. Developing agoraphobia is a fairly common side effect of coming off benzodiazepines – only one of a plethora of distressing psychological symptoms which may be brought on by withdrawal, as I was soon to see for myself.

Another person in my network of professional allies was Dr Lisa Brinkmann, a clinical psychologist and psychotherapist who had trained in her native Germany, in Hamburg, and had initially specialised in sex- and gender-related issues. Lisa had been living in Ireland since 2007. I told her what I was contemplating, and we agreed that I would go to her for a weekly session once I began withdrawal. I can honestly say that I do not know how I would have managed without those sessions, which we moved to twice weekly during the periods when things got very tough.

As for my personal support network at the time, this was very limited indeed. Only my mum was unwavering in her support, and only she seemed to have any real understanding of what I was trying to do, and why. For this, I will be forever grateful. Although a very sad thing to have to admit, the truth is that, apart from my mother and my daughter, the only other regular human contact I'd have in the time to come was from the professionals I paid to help me, and whom I was fortunate enough to be able to afford, even though the cost was not insignificant, and anyway, I felt I had no choice.

All this preparation might suggest that I was very much in control of the situation, and organised and clear-thinking in my approach. This wasn't the case at all. I'd always been good at research and quick to assimilate new information, as well as particularly interested in medical matters and alternative approaches to health, hence my discovery of the work of Professor Heather Ashton and my ability to see how it applied to my own situation. But I had to push myself very, very hard to find the energy to do what I needed to do: drawing up my personalised withdrawal schedule, creating a professional support network and trying to anticipate what might lie ahead. I was still living in a blur of mental fog and physical fatigue and could focus only with great difficulty and determination. I knew that the only way I could afford to approach this challenge was to regard it as being of life-or-death importance. And that indeed is what it turned out to be.

Twenty-One

The Dream

It's just Marie and me in the boat now all of the divers have gone down in sequence, tipping backwards into the beautiful, oily water in sets of two. Nic is partnered with Marie's husband, Ron. I've positioned the boat a little further west and have turned it round with the sun behind us, as is the usual protocol. This way we can keep watch for any divers coming to the surface without the sun in our eyes, which could obscure our view. Marie and I have been chatting about our experiences of pregnancy as she is also pregnant. Cheerily, I make my way below deck to go to the toilet, and I'm just unbolting the door of the little cubicle when I hear something from above deck. There's some kind of commotion and I can hear Marie calling me. I can't make out the words, but the urgency in her voice is unmistakable, and I hurry up to join her. As soon as she sees me, she points to the water.

'Rachel – there's someone in the water over there waving their arm.' I quickly take the wheel and slowly manoeuvre the boat alongside the waving diver – it's Ron.

His face is contorted with panic. 'It's Nic . . . He's lying on his back in the wreck's hold, and he's convulsing! He's having some kind of fit, it looks like!

'Quick, get on the radio, we need a chopper, get a chopper here fast! I tried to reach him, but I had to come up, I'd no choice – I lost my mouthpiece and weight belt while I was trying to help him, so I couldn't stay down. Quick, get help now!'

I immediately grab the radio handset, punch the channel 16 button and put out the international emergency call of Mayday, Mayday, Mayday. Immediately, the coast guard responds, and I begin to give details of my position and problem and request the assistance of the lifeboat and helicopter. At the same time, I rev the engines three times in the out-of-gear position to signal to any diver still down there that I have an emergency on the surface.

At that moment, just a few metres from Ron, I see a dark shadow looming beneath the water. There's a sudden rush of bubbles and water as another diver surfaces. My heart stops and I'm praying that it's Nic – that Ron has made a mistake and somehow misread the situation. But it's Paul, a regular diving buddy and friend. Registering the fear on our faces, he comes alongside. As he begins to take in what Ron is saying, he breaks in abruptly, 'I'm going back down', and begins to descend.

My blood is running cold: I don't, I can't, understand what is happening. One part of me registers the icy panic gripping my heart, and another Rachel, calm, deliberate, detached, takes over. She's the one who runs to the cabin looking for the oxygen bottle that will be needed for any resuscitation, who speaks to the coast guard, relaying our details and requesting an ambulance.

After what feels like an eternity but in reality is only seconds, the response comes back. '*Chopper is currently refuelling in Shannon and will be dispatched ASAP, ETA will be . . . Lifeboat being dispatched now – should be with you in twenty minutes, over—*'

'*Refuelling in Shannon*' – the detached part of me knows this is the last thing anyone hopes to hear when a diver is in trouble.

'No, no, no!' I call back. 'If we can retrieve the diver, we will steam ashore ASAP – request an ambulance and doctor to assist at Union Hall Pier! – over.'

'*Baltimore lifeboat has launched. ETA now less than ten minutes . . . Standing by.*'

The radio exchanges continued as I waited to see the lifeboat come into view and stared through the wheelhouse window, trying to magic Nic to the surface.

Now without a point of focus, all my fear, all my dread, takes over. Where is Nic? Where is my husband, the father of my unborn child? Please, please God, please let him be okay.

◆   ◆   ◆

The crossover from Frisium to Valium was very, very rough. I was aiming to transition from taking 10mg of Frisium three times a day to 15mgs of Valium once a day, as advised in the *Ashton Manual*. I'd drawn up a carefully considered schedule, setting out each day's dosage, beginning by adding in very small doses of Valium with a corresponding reduction of my usual dose of Frisium, and continuing until I'd phased out the Frisium and was taking only Valium. Before I started, I read a lot on the Benzo Buddies forums about other people's experiences of drug substitution and transitioning and thought I had some idea of what to expect. But nothing could have prepared me for the rollercoaster of the three weeks it took to complete the crossover.

The dream about the scene of Nic's death was only one of the recurring nightmares to assail me during the very short periods each night when I managed to fall asleep. I also relived in vivid Technicolor the final weeks of Dominic's life as the cancer decimated his body. Then there was the persistent image of my father's face as he looked disdainfully at Dominic's lifeless body and muttered something inaudible, an oddly triumphant look in his eyes. I relived the night of the day Nic died, when Nicky had brought me back to my house. Lauraine had gently undressed me and helped me into the bath, where I sat, rigid and upright, in uncomprehending desolation. Gazing down at the swell of my belly, I could not fathom how I was going to love and care for the baby within me when they emerged into a world where Nic no longer had a place.

Without the cushioning, numbing filters of the benzos my system had relied on for so long, every single unprocessed trauma I had ever lived through came roaring back with a force and intensity no human being should ever have to endure. Stripped of everything, infinitely vulnerable, like an animal flayed alive, all my psyche could do was curl into a self-protective ball and hope to somehow survive the storm.

If my nights were lived in the clutch of relentless anxiety, my days were dominated by a proliferation of bizarre and frightening physical sensations and symptoms. The first time I made the short journey to see Lisa Brinkmann, my therapist, after starting the crossover to Valium, I was gripped by the oddest impressions as I tried to walk down the street. It felt as if everything had suddenly taken on gigantic proportions. The road seemed three miles wide, the shop windows shrank strangely back from me as I passed by. Suddenly my body was outsized, ungainly; now I was seven feet tall, and my arms and legs gangled before me, like flailing branches on a tree being buffeted in a storm. My head seemed huge and bulbous, swelling out above my neck like a balloon. Everyone was staring at me; I was being covertly observed from every direction – from behind curtains and in the rear-view mirrors of parked cars. Passers-by seemed to glare at me, looking me up and down with contempt and flinching in disgust as they did so. By the time I arrived at Lisa's rooms, I was terrified. And within a matter of days, I was in the grip of severe agoraphobia.

Somehow, during those weeks, I stuck doggedly to my tapering regime. I forced myself to honour my appointments with Lisa, and I managed to get to my osteopathy appointments. As well as the odd visual distortions I was experiencing, I found myself at the mercy of an ever-changing succession of extreme moods – from rage and vitriol at everything and everyone, to fits of sobbing, despair and grey sadness. I was powerless to moderate or control it in any way. Along with the awful lows came fear – visceral, dark fear.

I lived for the daily visits of my mum, which became the one reliable point of reference in my day; Mum would never fail to turn up when she said she would. Yet even though I waited anxiously for her arrival, from the time she came in the front door until she left again an hour or two later, I spent every moment sobbing inconsolably or raging uncontrollably. It must have been incredibly difficult for her to see me so distraught, but she would stay calm and often simply listened, bearing witness to my suffering without judging or trying to fight against what I was going through. In doing this, she provided me with a vital safety valve, giving me for that short time an outlet for all my overwhelming feelings. To this day I am convinced that in this way she helped to save my life.

During the long hours alone, I would weep or rage for hours, but so often this felt futile and, of course, unheard. There is something about having someone close to you hear and acknowledge your suffering that can somehow alleviate it, even if that's not always how it feels at the time, or you don't understand until much later what a difference it made to you. I believe that this is how humans are wired, and that this is a very important part of how healing can take place: to have connection and to have witness to our suffering.

Twenty-Two

The Dream

Here it comes again: that terrible image . . . Stark, absolute, impossible to misinterpret – an image that will stay burned into my memory. It is grotesque, a freeze frame from a horror movie.

I'm on the boat again, out at sea on that high-summer evening. Except I can no longer see the light of the golden evening sun or feel the warm air on my skin – it is cold, so cold, only cold. I'm looking over the side of the boat, my eyes fixed on the surface of the water, waiting, waiting, with bated breath and a sense of dread. Marie and Ron are beside me. None of us can take our eyes from the water.

Now I see a dark form looming fast towards the surface. It must be a diver – another of the guys from the group, or even, possibly, Nic. *Could it be Nic?*

Heralded by a rush of bubbles, the shape finally breaks the surface. And now I can see clearly, unforgettably, that no, it's not one of the other divers. But it can't be Nic either. It just can't be. It's an inert, lifeless mass, bobbing now on the water. It's someone's body; they're lying on their back, like a starfish, arms outstretched, legs splayed, body encased in a neoprene suit. The diver's mask has been removed, and the mouthpiece floats from a hose in the water beside them; the eyes are open but blank, expressionless.

How can it be Nic? Or if it is, it can't be real. As the image imprints itself on to my brain, at the same time its meaning is completely beyond me. I'm staring in bewilderment, just staring, when the surface of the ocean is broken once more and another form comes to the surface close by. This time, I recognise them. It's Paul again, Nic's friend.

'I found him – in the hold of the wreck, at about 30 metres. He was just lying there, his mouthpiece out, not moving. So I pressed his emergency inflation button, to get him to the surface.'

There is a flurry of movement to get Nic on board. Ron, Marie and another diver grab hold of the inert body and begin to pull. But despite their efforts, and Paul's from the side of the boat, Nic's body seems to resist being hauled on to the deck. So, while part of me stays staring in disbelief, the other part springs into motion again, pushing myself in between Ron and Marie, to grab on to one of the limbs and add my strength to theirs as they tug and tug. I'm six months pregnant, but from somewhere I find a kind of superhuman strength and, together, we are finally able to haul the body on to the boat. It slumps on to the deck alongside us until it is lying prone once more, at our feet now.

I quickly tip back the head, open the mouth and try to blow into the lungs, and then stop. I walk away. There's a strange gur-gling sound in the lungs, but then nothing, nothing at all, and the body continues to lie there, inert. I've looked at the face and into the dear eyes so familiar to me, and I know, now, that it is Nic, my Nic. It's impossible to pretend any longer that it isn't him.

As the others spring into action – mouth to mouth, CPR, oxygen – I walk away again. I grab the radio and begin to update the coast guard. 'We've got him on deck now. Where's the lifeboat? And what's the ETA for the chopper?!'

Now audible on the still air, the *thrum thrum* of the lifeboat's powerful twin engines throbs across the sea towards me. In no time they are with us and pull alongside. I see John Breen in his RNLI uniform, another friend and diver, come on board and within a short time he is in the wheelhouse in front of me.

'No, John, it's not me – it's Nic, there's something wrong with him! Go and see, we've got to save him. We've got to get the chopper here as soon as we possibly can.'

John's face is so grim; he just looks at me and gently says, 'Rachel, I'm so sorry.' In that moment, it was as if my brain split. On one level I know what he means, and on another I don't want to know, so I just stare back at him and hear myself saying, 'How's Nic?' It's as if I've been cleaved in two. I just ask him to keep working on my Nic. I feel my belly undulate and, all of a sudden, I feel very, very old.

◆　◆　◆

Almost five years later, in the spring of 2003, an inquest was held into Nic's death in order to finally determine what exactly had gone wrong that day. Richard, the wonderful solicitor who later pursued the case against the Cromwell hospital for my medical costs, had advised that there may be liability on the part of the company that manufactured the rebreather equipment Nic was using the day he died. The hearing went on for several days, during which time a great deal of evidence was put forward for the coroner's consideration, including statements from ten witnesses, the pathologist and AP Valves, later renamed Ambient Pressure Diving, the manufacturers of Nic's diving equipment, the highly sophisticated and then new-to-market 'Buddy Inspiration Rebreather'. The company's representatives were trying to suggest that Nic's death had been due to his own negligence.

The pathologist was able to confirm that Nic drowned after a 'metabolic incident' which had led to him losing consciousness; a technical expert who examined the gear after the event reported that both of the handsets attached to the gear, which contained vital electronic equipment to monitor gas levels, were cracked and full of sea water. After much back and forth, the jury returned an open verdict, which effectively absolved Nic of any allegations of negligence for his own death. Although AP Valves were loath to accept this conclusion, I felt that I had vindicated Nic's reputation as a very experienced and responsible scuba diver.

Twenty-Three

2011–2012

> . . . *I cannot even imagine for one second feeling at ease or enjoying myself . . . What is enjoyment? Mostly I simply endure; I just try to get through the days. Did you know that even the chickens are stressful? It is only once they are fed and put to bed that I can let go of the awful tension. Then a break, until I must cook dinner, and suffer more . . . I have to keep it very simple now, because my obsession about washing pots takes away any desire to make something more elaborate. It's such a burden to wash up, but if I avoid doing it, the suffering is worse. Is this what the rest of the world calculates before embarking on the evening meal? The washing-up is done? I honestly don't know any more . . .*

When your world has shrunk to the narrowest of confines – the four walls of your home and the decreasing circles of a mind perhaps irrevocably damaged by medication – the tiniest everyday tasks can seem gargantuan. Ancient wisdom teaches us that true contentment can lie in the simplest of things, but when you are wrestling with physical addiction and, perhaps, incipient mental illness, these small things can cause unimaginable anguish.

For many months, as I continued the struggle to break my physical dependence on benzodiazepines, my daily life was dominated by the life-or-death necessity of completing three simple tasks – feeding the chickens, cooking dinner for Nicola and myself, and, perhaps most daunting of all, doing the washing-up. As farcical as it seems now, with each new day I had to 'screw my courage to the sticking place' (in the words of Lady Macbeth) and muster up all of my mental and physical energy to get through these basic routines. Only then could I allow myself a short respite from the visceral anxiety that the thought of not completing them would set in motion.

Until that point, keeping chickens was something I'd always enjoyed. I'd loved the rituals of feeding them, scattering the grain and changing the water and then, in the early evening, 'putting them to bed', making sure that they were all accounted for and locked up safely in their coop for the night. The best ritual of all was the daily or twice-daily visit into the dim coolness of the hen-house to inspect the nests, feeling for the warm ovals of freshly laid eggs. I'd always kept a few chickens to be able to enjoy the pleasure of free-range eggs and the diverting antics of these funny birds. But now, from early afternoon onwards, I thought of the chickens with dread. Looking after them was just one more way I had to engage with a reality I couldn't bear; one more irksome task to be completed before I could finally sign off on another bleak day and go to bed.

In a similar vein, as an adult, I'd always loved cooking, and food has always been a passion. This meant I was able to stand in when I had to for the resident chef in The Pier House bistro when I was in my early twenties. I loved to choose the best fresh local ingredients which would really showcase the fantastic seafood we'd get delivered directly from the boats each day. But the person I was now, struggling simply to get through to the next minute, was unrecognisable. Now, my life was ruled by my morbid, compulsive obsession with the washing-up and keeping at bay the awful fear that would threaten to engulf me if I did not deal with the dishes. Otherwise, the dirty saucepans and used plates would sit on the side of the sink like a terrible reproach, a reminder of everything I'd ever done wrong in my life.

Yet, if I managed to stick to the tapering schedule, those bleak days when I was 'simply enduring' were in many ways the positive ones. Although I did allow myself to have 'holding' periods, when I waited for an extra week or several weeks before instating the next dose reduction, not once did I 'go backwards', as they term it in the *Ashton Manual*, and decide to return to a higher dose. Nor did I resort to the 'escape pills' which some doctors advocate – antidepressants to get over the hump of a particularly stressful event or time. So, in that sense, I was always making progress of some kind, always moving forwards. Not that, in that period, I would have had the perspective to recognise this, let alone the ability to give myself any kind of credit for it – or for anything else, for that matter.

But every two weeks, as I made another incremental reduction in my Valium dosage, there was a fresh hell to be lived through, especially for the first few days, as my body took the hit and battled to adjust. By the end of the fortnight, I would just about be finding a little equilibrium again (although I use the term very lightly), when it would be time to make the next cut. For several months, although I might have been experiencing some tiny, gradual overall improvements, at the time I had no awareness of this; as far as I could see, I was just living in different levels of hell at any one time – nothing that approached normality, let alone calm or contentment. And it was always the night-times I struggled with the most. Of course, in many ways, this had been the case since my surgery years previously, when sleep had first begun to elude me in a serious way.

But the nights during those times when I'd just introduced another cut to my dose could be the most brutal of all . . .

I have just put behind me one of the most horrific nights in a long time. The depths of my despair had me talking out loud in the darkness for hours. I just couldn't contain the horror within my skull any longer. I wanted to die there and then, and get away from the body which is supposed to be my home.

How can life have such dark places within it that the only option left is to contemplate a quick end? The absolute dread that I live with makes me feel separate from all mankind, as if I am a human misfit. I can hardly find words to describe the pits that I descended to last night. I begged God to take me and end my suffering. This awful evil chatter, coupled with these black, black thoughts . . . But I'm too cowardly to end it, plus I still harbour the hope that I might one day get to live in peace.

Eternal peace is what I crave. So why do I fear death so much, then? It is a black, slim, evil ward for the existential suffering on this plane. And I don't win either way. I love Nicola. I don't want to make her hate me or cause her more suffering. She is all I have to show for my pitiful life . . . God . . . let it be over . . . I give up.

The drug withdrawal period was the first time that suicide entered my mind. Even when Dominic died, even when I lost Nic, I'd never thought about killing myself. Yes, sometimes, I had wanted to die.

Especially in the days and months after Nic's accident, I'd thought about how much easier it would be to not have to be alive any more. Sometimes I longed so much to be with him again. Not only had I fantasised about joining him in death, but I'd imagined that it might have been better if I'd been there on the seabed with him that day, if we had both died there; we could simply drift off together, borne away by the element in which we both felt so at home. But I never reached the point of thinking seriously about ending it all. Apart from anything else, the arrival of Nicola had kept me tethered to this earth, and especially in the first few years, the demands of motherhood kept me firmly in the present, without the mental or physical energy to contemplate being anywhere else. And when it came down to it, at this latest point in my life, when I was trying to kick the benzos, it was the thought of Nicola that stopped me crossing that line. My love for her was ultimately stronger and more visceral than my longing for death. But sometimes, only just.

From my frequent daily visits to the Benzo Buddies forums, I knew that many people going through this kind of withdrawal experience regular and persistent thoughts of suicide. Indeed, incredibly sadly, within the short space of time since I'd joined the online community, several forum members had succumbed to those dark thoughts and, tragically, ended their lives.

Whenever the 'black, slimy, evil' thoughts of killing myself began to pervade my mind, I was somehow able to sit with them. Don't ask me how, but I was able to stay just that tiniest bit separate from them. I could see them. They almost had personalities – a council of advisors and persuaders – and it took all my might not to listen. It felt like I was locked in a battle between good and evil. I had to be on my guard around the clock. I didn't really want to be dead, I just wanted the suffering to be over.

But as the bleak diary entry above says, '*I still harbour the hope that I might one day get to live in peace . . .*' Something else was holding me back from crossing the final line between life and death; something that had always been in me and which kept me engaged. In the most difficult moments of my childhood, in the times I felt most alone and sad and, later, when Dominic and then Nic were gone, it was always there, like an infinitesimal chink of light at the very end of a dark and tortuous tunnel. This was the belief that life held something better for me, for all of us. Suffering, pain and separation are not all there is. On balance, the good things – the benevolent energy, the positive, beautiful life force that infuses the natural world around us and the universe itself – are stronger than everything else. But, of course, I wouldn't realise the truth of this for a long, long time.

Meanwhile, as well as all the emotional and psychological suffering it brought, the physical effects of benzo withdrawal were waging war on my body. Keeping a diary was something that had been suggested on the Benzo Buddies forums as a helpful way of keeping tabs on any progress over the longer term, which might not always be discernible when you are immersed in the daily struggle of withdrawal. Looking back at that diary, I can see that I've registered no fewer than forty-seven different symptoms that I experienced on a regular basis throughout those long months.

Of these, one of the most persistent and difficult to manage was an assortment of chronic and sometimes bizarre issues with my skin which ramped up my nightly insomnia to an unbearable degree. As a direct result of benzo withdrawal, my skin was constantly breaking out into large, burning, weeping, raw patches all over my body. These were maddeningly itchy and, when scratched, became even more itchy, causing me to tear at my skin constantly. The itching was at its worst at night, and no matter what I tried – Piriton tablets, preparations and ointments and heavy-duty steroid creams – nothing seemed to ease it. Persistent night sweats only compounded the problem. Searing pain in my back and coccyx caused me to stutter in pain when getting up or sitting down, and I would regularly get painful ulcers in my mouth.

As well as all of this, I had persistent bowel and bladder problems: agonising bouts of IBS-like symptoms, constipation and chronic bladder irritation. I'd be driven to get up to pee ten or more times a night. Sometimes there was very little to pass, and others I'd pass up to five litres a night. I had a swollen face and bloated belly (colloquially known as 'benzo belly'), and my ankles and calves were thick and spongy with fluid retention. Basically, my body was in meltdown. I suffered, I raged, I wept and I endured twenty-four hours a day, seven days a week.

Periodically I also found myself at the mercy of a wide range of horrendous symptoms which had both physical and psychological effects. For example, at night I suffered from a constant, unbearable sense of restlessness and a complete inability to stay still. I soon learned that this was what doctors refer to as 'akathisia': a syndrome characterised by an inability to remain in a sitting or lying posture with 'motor restlessness and a feeling of muscular quivering'. Akathisia is another widely recognised side effect of some common psychotropic drugs. For me, this also manifested itself in sudden twitches and painful, bolting, electrical-like zaps all over my body, particularly in my spine, or indeed the sudden, shocking jolting of my entire body. It would happen especially at night, often when I was on the verge of sleep, meaning that I'd be jerked into wakefulness and the full awareness again of the misery of my physical symptoms. The restlessness was both a physical sensation and a psychological state; just as my body could find no peace, so my mind kept turning over and over in increasingly negative 'thought loops'.

It is almost impossible to convey to those who haven't experienced this what it is like to inhabit a mind where every single waking thought is a negative one. Much later, as I progressed in the withdrawal process, I would learn to make the crucial distinction between my thoughts and the person that I was – and to realise that, no matter how compelling my thoughts were, I didn't have to listen to them and had the power to distinguish between those that were helpful and those that were not. However, in the early stages of withdrawal, I found myself utterly at the mercy of a relentlessly negative and cruel inner voice. The negativity would engulf me, not only in the form of individual, separate thoughts, but also in a set of endlessly recurring themes which modulated constantly in my head, in obsessive, futile cycles.

One of these was the contrast between the person I had been in the past and the person I felt myself to be now. I obsessed endlessly over how capable and full of life I had been before, and compared this with the sad, mute, desperately lonely woman I was now, someone who was quite literally afraid to venture beyond her own doorstep. But rather than seeing the comparison as a source of reassurance – something along the lines of 'If this is what I was like in the past, I can get back to it again in the future' – my mind used it as a means of further torture, as I berated myself for the depths I'd allowed myself to sink to. I regarded my old self as being from another life – one that was over now, and to which I could never return. An extract from my journal at the time sums up this sense of despair and powerlessness very well:

> I'm not sure of who I am, I'm really not. My mind's eye throws up the image of a bubbly beauty of a ball of blonde pressured up by the joy of connecting with another being; the feeling that I had enough of me to go around; always ready with a laugh and an acknowledgement of you, of the other [person]. . .

> I was not mundane – quite the opposite. But now I'm grey, just grey. I've lost my plumage; I've lost my sheen and

I am one of those black-and-white photos of the ages . . .
I'm a shadow looking at my own ghost speaking – how
did it get to this? I want my sparkle back, I want my
voice. Instead it's the tone of feet on stone, dull, dense,
without any resonance.

But still I kept going, somehow, in the way I always had, doggedly putting one foot in front of the other. Fourteen months into withdrawal, I was down to taking just 0.5mg of Valium. This was a massive reduction from my starting point of 15mg, and something even I was able to acknowledge was a huge achievement. But I would have no time to rest on my laurels. A matter of days after I made the latest cut to my dose, the thing I'd been dreading most finally happened. I had a massive seizure and, in the absence of any immediate medical support and in absolute fear, I upped my dose of Valium at once, back to 10mg. After a year and three months of relentless struggle, I was nearly right back at the beginning again.

Twenty-Four

The Dream

Another image I will never forget.

I am still on the deck of our boat, but now it's a hive of activity, crowded with people, equipment, divers and Royal National Lifeboat crew running back and forth. All the eleven other divers are back on board. Some are still dismantling their gear, others simply standing still or sitting down, stunned and shaken, their bowed heads in their hands. The lifeboat crew move up and down the deck, calling out instructions to one another. They've been working on Nic, doing CPR, I presume, for what seems like a lifetime, and now, finally, the helicopter has arrived. It screeches in the sky above us, its sweeping blades deafening us, their whirring motion creating a sickening scudding on the surface of the water. There's spray everywhere. The lifeboat crew, used to the procedure, are readying the deck for the winch man above to descend to the boat from the now hovering Sikorsky helicopter.

I see that Nic is laid out on the deck in front of me and that the winch man is crouching over his body, examining him, while some of the lifeboat guys look on, shouting to one another through cupped ears and shaking their heads. Now it looks like they're attaching a harness to Nic, under his arms and around his chest, and I'm assuming they're getting him ready to be strapped into a stretcher of some kind, so that they can airlift him to the nearest hospital. As I watch, I'm willing them to hurry, hurry.

They're taking Nic to hospital – I'm going with him. I want to go with him – they have to take me too. 'Please, I need to go with Nic . . .'

No one responds to my words. Instead, everyone – John, Ron, Marie, the other divers – falls silent and bows their head.

Someone comes close, finally, and shouts, 'The lifeboat guys will be taking you – you're to go with them. One of us will bring the boat in after you.'

'But why can't I go with Nic in the chopper? And why's he not even on a stretcher or anything?' I look around, appealing for help and intervention.

'Rachel, you can't go in the chopper. You're pregnant and it's not safe for you . . . You go with the lifeboat, now.'

'But—'

And in that moment, I see the winch man ready himself to lift. Nic's lifeless body begins to lift with him and, coupled together, they begin to rise skywards. Slowly, its huge engines thundering, the helicopter starts to rise further into the sky, vertically at first, until it's high, high above. Then the nose dips slightly and the craft swings forward as it heads landwards. I look up and in that split second I see Nic hanging below the roaring aircraft, suspended from a sling looped around his chest. As the chopper climbs and then sweeps away towards the shore, his inert body disappears upwards and inside as they make their way east and to land. A great, rending grief rips through my heart as I watch my husband, my dear Nic, being spirited away, higher and more distant with each moment. He is gone, and there's nothing I can do but watch the black dot disappear.

Twenty-Five

September 2012

It's hard to put into words the worst episode of this whole period. That it happened at all makes me deeply sad even today, though the flip side is that at least now I can see it for what it was and have compassion for the person I'd become. I was just so very ill.

Sitting on the stairs one day in my little farmhouse, my head was filled with what I can only describe as 'voices' telling me, gently, that if I was going to end my life, my precious daughter and mother should come with me. The idea that I might kill them as well as myself took shape slowly, yet as a perfectly 'normal' thing to contemplate. If I was to go, the two people I loved most would need to come with me. It was the only way. In my tortured mind, a battle began to rage between good and evil, between horror that I was thinking this way and the feeling that it was the natural, loving thing to do. I battled, I spoke aloud, I agreed, I argued, I reasoned, I won, I lost. And on it went. I weep now at my helplessness in a war between a mind that was very ill and that tiny part of me that still knew what was right and what true love really was. Hours slipped by, and the light changed, as I fought with myself. I still remember my voice almost shouting: 'No! I won't listen to you, I don't believe you, people who love don't kill.' It took all my emotional strength to silence this awful idea, and steadily I began to win. But it left me utterly shaken, my mind shredded at the notion that these feelings might assault me, catch me off guard, in the future. Thankfully, this was not a battle I ever had to face again. My gorgeous Nicola and amazing mother were safe.

◆ ◆ ◆

The world, to me, was full of pain; everywhere, people were suffering unbearable physical pain and mental agony. There was no respite, no escape – we were all condemned to eke out our lives in despair. Only death would bring some kind of release.

In the previous few weeks, I'd become absolutely convinced of the truth of all of this. It had begun one morning at dawn, when I'd had yet another sleepless night and had lain there, the curtains open, dreading the arrival of the first signs of light and the sinking horror I knew I'd feel at the sound of birdsong. My thoughts had turned to the world outside: I was all too conscious that there was an abattoir only a few miles from my house. As someone brought up in a rural community, I knew that killing livestock was part and parcel of rearing animals for market, but, from my early teenage years, I was haunted by the idea of it. The thought of the countless animals we routinely slaughter every day made me feel sick and full of panic. In these last bleak months, I'd become increasingly and morbidly preoccupied by the fate of these animals and, specifically, of the animals herded together within the walls of the abattoir, waiting to be killed. I couldn't bear the thought of any of it, and deep in the night and in the early mornings, I was convinced I could hear the shrieks of terror from the assembled pigs as they witnessed others being slaughtered and sensed that their own deaths were imminent. I couldn't escape these sounds in my head. A hostage to my own wayward mind, I felt personally responsible for the suffering of these poor creatures. That I was part of the society that had brought them into the world to die to fulfil our needs tormented me and, in these desolate hours, it was as if I had become just another animal myself.

Looking back, it's clear that this – the period in which I felt homicidal as well as suicidal – was the lowest point in my second attempt to wean myself off benzodiazepines. After my seizure in May 2012, when I'd had to resume Valium at a higher dose again, I'd taken the rest of the summer to get myself stabilised and in a place where I didn't feel in imminent danger of suffering further seizures. Of course, I was bitterly disappointed that I hadn't managed to say goodbye to the Valium altogether, especially when I'd been so close to doing so, but I also knew that I had little choice but to stabilise on this dose and begin the weaning process all over again. By September 2012, I'd duly rallied myself to start the withdrawal process once more.

Once more I can only be grateful that I was able to find that tiny part of me that was still functional and fight my broken mind. There was no quick fix, but somehow I managed to keep anchored enough throughout a period when I can honestly say that I'd lost my mind completely. My often twice-weekly visits to Lisa, my therapist, and my mother's daily trips to see me helped me to download just enough emotional pressure, until gradually, slowly, I no longer felt the urge to kill my loved ones – or myself.

It was not just the work with Lisa that helped me, however. Since my first attempt at withdrawal began, at the end of 2010, I was now physically strong enough to take up yoga. Initially, I'd have short one-to-one yoga therapy classes with Jessica once a week and, in time, when I was strong enough and my paranoia would allow it, I attended her regular group sessions. I also began my own daily practice at home, for at least an hour and a half at a time. Meditation became a key part of my routine. No matter how I was feeling or how extreme things got, I doggedly kept to these simple routines and, over time, they helped me immensely.

At the beginning, the yoga was remedial, designed to help me work on areas of my body where my movement remained limited, as well as target my powers of physical coordination more generally, which were still badly compromised. Once I began to make good progress in the remedial work, Jessica began to shift the focus to the practice of Yin yoga. Yin yoga is a slower, more nuanced form of yoga where poses are typically held for between two and five minutes – much longer than in the more dynamic, faster-moving Vinyasa yoga which most people associate with the practice. Each posture in Yin yoga targets the body's fascia, aiming to stretch and smooth these in order to release damaging tension and to restore balance to the body at a very deep level. Fascia is the connective tissue which wraps around muscles and organs, offering support and minimising friction during the body's everyday movements. Recent scientific findings have confirmed the principle at the heart of Yin yoga: that if the fascia are damaged, under stress or tightly contracted, our physical and mental well-being are negatively affected; and that stretching and increasing the blood flow within the fascia will improve our overall health and sense of well-being, by easing chronic pain and restoring alignment and mobility to muscles and joints.

Since Yin yoga targets deep-seated problems in the body which may have existed for a very long time, it is a practice that requires patience and, understandably, takes time for dramatic results to be felt. But even early on in my sessions, I was aware of benefits and small improvements to the way I was feeling and instinctively felt that the practice was right for me. Jessica explained that one of the key principles is that we should aim to step just beyond our comfort zone each time we practise, and that for this reason the work might at times feel slightly, or even intensely, uncomfortable, as the body learns to relax into the stretches and the fascia extend and smooth themselves, although, of course, as she warned, we should never work through any significant degree of pain. It is not unusual, especially once a regular practice is established, to feel a corresponding sense of emotional release.

All of this made perfect sense to me, and soon I began to feel the more profound effects of our Yin yoga work, which encouraged me to keep up my own daily sessions at home. As I did this, I was able to achieve a deeper understanding of the physical and psychological aspects to the practice and how they are interlinked. As time went on, I learned to use my Yin yoga practice as a way of healing past emotional wounds, by taking the principle of gradually extending my physical limits and applying this to the memories and feelings generated in me by past traumas, which inhabited not only my mind but also my body, at a deep, cellular level. Gradually I grew more confident in my practice and my belief in its benefits, and increasingly I was able to sit with whatever memories and emotions came up for me, and do so from a standpoint of safety and with greater faith in my own resilience as an adult. I could relive and acknowledge the pain I'd felt as a child, teenager or young woman, and offer compassion and forgiveness to myself, in the assurance that I was now strong enough to look after the most vulnerable, damaged parts of myself in the way a good parent would.

Meditation, too, struck a very deep chord, as a way of feeling more anchored and as a 'coming home' to myself. The practice of always returning to the breath – first the inhale and then the exhale – gave me a sense of grounding that grew and strengthened the more I practised. Years later, I would realise that the experience is very much akin to that of diving: utter silence, deep calm and a profound sense of freedom, along with an edge of the unknown.

As I learned more and read more about meditation, I became progressively drawn to the philosophy of Buddhism and began to read extensively about it. My interest in Buddhism was not entirely new. Throughout my childhood, my mum would sometimes talk about Buddhist beliefs and how they appealed to her, the suggestion being that somehow this religion was also right for me. At the time, she didn't take those ideas any further in her own life. My guess is that she was too caught up in the more pressing problems of the situation she was in, looking after five children in a remote part of Ireland, a place where she knew she didn't belong, with a much older husband who was mostly difficult, controlling and coercive.

Twenty-Six

Winter 2012

One of the valuable self-defence mechanisms of the human psyche is the way it seeks to prevent us from continually reliving the most painful times of the past. It does this by allowing us, with the passing of months and years, to let go of the intensity of the feelings and sensations we had at the time. Today, I can't easily recall in detail the daily suffering of the long months of my second attempt at withdrawal. In these chapters I've tried to elaborate on the depths to which I fell, but, thankfully, many of my memories have faded in the intervening years. During the final stages of the process, from November 2012 to May 2013, I did, however, keep a consistent, almost daily diary of sorts, unlike earlier, when I just jotted things down in an ad hoc way. This record has been invaluable in helping me see the bigger picture, as my body adapted to coping with smaller and smaller quantities of Valium, until finally, on 27 May 2013, I was able to take my very last tablet.

When I read through my 'withdrawal diary' today, I can now identify a broader process of healing. This is clear not just in the gradual diminishing of my physical withdrawal symptoms, but in crucial emotional and psychological terms too. This process of recovery culminated in what I can only describe now as a spiritual breakthrough – a period of intense growth and learning which, to me, finally made sense of all the suffering I'd had to endure to that point. This realisation – that I was on a journey so difficult it almost killed me, but which has led me to the place of joyful gratitude I inhabit today – still has the power to move and inspire me, because I maintain it's a journey of which all of us are capable. My own experience, personal and professional, has taught me to truly believe that inherent in each of us is a core strength that when required reveals itself. It is often only when we have truly reached rock bottom that it can appear, but it's there nevertheless.

◆ ◆ ◆

In a journal entry of early November 2012, I set down my thoughts on a recent session with Lisa in which we began to identify and challenge some of my most long-held and damaging beliefs about myself and about life itself:

> *Had discussion with Lisa about brain damage and my limitations as a person. About how to let go of the expectations of a life where I am healed, and how to begin living in acceptance of today as it is. Accepting that I will never be as I was pre-surgery, and that I have a fragility that needs to be cared for and respected . . .*

> *. . . Acceptance is not something that I really understand. The guilt of not having achieved enough or feeling that I have not tried harder is always running as a second voice within my mind. It lives with me 24/7 and keeps me locked in a world of guilt and self-loathing. This inner voice is so desperately unkind and, coupled with*

the distortion of the benzo dependency, means that I live
in my own mini-world of hell, constantly . . .

The work with Lisa was bringing me face to face with some of the most problematic issues in how I had been living my life until this point. Over the weeks that followed, as my diary entries show, I continued to struggle with the idea of acknowledging and accepting the reality of my situation and the need to let go of the impossible standards to which I'd always held myself. I began to see how the perfectionistic traits I'd adopted since my earliest childhood had become self-defeating and, ultimately, self-destructive. And I was forced to confront the fact that the only way forward – the only way for me to continue living at all – was to accept my limitations and be kinder to myself:

> *It hurt to hear those words, 'brain damage', but it's been a relief of sorts too . . . Almost like having a label, a diagnosis. Somehow that makes me feel more valid. I've no real understanding of the mental battle I'm holding every day, but I know it's exhausting. I'm fighting to stay alive a lot of the time. I don't really have any comfort in my head. It's all negative talk, all the time, and even through the night. It's as if part of me doesn't like me and is doing its best to destroy every minute I exist . . . It's horrible, never-ending and unbearable . . .*

As the days stretched into late November and then early December, I continued to have many lows and to suffer from the entrenched withdrawal symptoms of chronic insomnia, anxiety, emotional volatility and physical discomfort. But in parallel to this, as my diary entries show, I was making important progress in terms of gaining insight and a far greater level of self-awareness. What is fascinating to me now is that in this hard-won wisdom I can see the very beginnings of the awareness which informs so much of my work as a therapist today, as I strive to help clients heal from trauma and achieve personal transformation. It is clear from my journal too that, based on my own lived experience, I was in the process of forming some of the key insights which lie at the heart of the science of epigenetics, which proposes that the internal environment we create for our bodies and minds has the power to influence our physical and mental health.

> *I see my brain cells taking on the burden [of my negative thoughts] and the image of them getting greyer and more permeable becomes more distinct . . . So I spend a lot of my time bargaining with my cells. If I think good thoughts, will that help? Trying to think good thoughts in my current condition is such a strain, because I imagine my subconscious is not fooled and carries on making my body sick behind the scenes. However, on my good days I just try to do this on a very practical level: I construct a happy thought and I simply keep repeating it to my inner self, hoping that perhaps in this way I can fool it . . .*

3 December 2012

As the New Year began, I was still fluctuating between very dark moods and a stability of sorts, albeit the stability of an emotional flat line, with little sense of connection to other people or ability to truly relate to everyday trials and triumphs:

> *I can't feel much apart from the most extreme emotions . . . It needs to be a car crash or such for me to grasp at an emotion. It hurts because I know it's not*

'normal'. . . Living with this terrible great blank makes
connecting so difficult . . .

3 January 2013 (3.5mg Valium)

Adding to this sense of being apart from the world and the people in it was the severe insomnia I continued to suffer from most nights. There are few places more lonely in the world than when you're lying in bed alone at 4 a.m., having not yet slept and knowing that sleep will probably elude you for long hours to come:

> *My shadow feels like the inmate of an asylum. My eyes look out from these grey windows: I am trapped. I pray for sleep but it will come only in its own time, according to a schedule which I am never privy to, and all I can do is wait. I'm very polite to it, really. I just get my book and settle myself to wait/pass the time . . . Hours later and slowly, so slowly, it drapes itself around my shoulders . . . Not letting me escape into oblivion until I have suffered further jolting and twitching and more pain . . .*

As the weeks passed, however, incrementally (in the same way sleep would finally come to me, in its own time and according to its own schedule), I began to experience small improvements to the quality of my everyday life. Very importantly too, by the end of January 2013, I was able to travel to Dublin – by train and then bus – to take part in a five-day Buddhist silent retreat being held by some Buddhist monks from the Plum Village, the exiled home of the great spiritual leader, Thich Nhat Hanh. I'd been reading more and more about Buddhism at this time, and in the preceding few months had been devouring the books of Thich Nhat Hanh and following the daily feeds on the website of Plum Village, near

Bordeaux in France: the first Buddhist monastic community set up by Hanh in the West.

His teachings and thinking, and the focus on the breath and the practice of mindfulness, resonated with me profoundly, and when I'd read about the retreat, I was determined to go. This was a huge step out of my comfort zone. I hadn't stayed away from home at all for more than a few hours in the previous two years, since the beginning of withdrawal, in fact, and the prospect of travelling alone on public transport to an unfamiliar environment, with a group of strangers on a silent retreat, was intimidating and scary, to say the least. While I was beginning to feel a little better, I was still pitifully vulnerable and unsure of myself. But just as I was determined to push my body beyond its limits of comfort in every session of my yoga practice, I knew that the time had come to extend myself in other ways too.

The first two days on the retreat were very challenging. Since I was a complete novice when it came to monastic retreats and their etiquette, I didn't realise at first that the way everyone greeted each other – waving both hands – was the customary approach on silent retreats of this kind. In my paranoia, I assumed that the others all knew each other from prior meetings and that I was the only true newcomer. Over time I realised what the form was and didn't feel quite so marginalised.

To start off with too, I found it very difficult to sit in community. I was so used to being alone – my inner monologue was relentless and invariably negative. For the first forty-eight hours, I just could not subdue the constant mental chatter in my mind, and at night it continued without respite. On the third day, however, my mind began to clear and become a little quieter until, almost miraculously, the usual relentless train of circular thinking slowed, and then simply stopped, for longer and longer intervals. By day five, I was occupying an entirely new mental space – one with periods of relative calm and a new sense of simply existing, of just being in the moment. For the first time in my life, I felt I'd been able to access a peaceful inner core to my being which I'd never suspected was there – and yet somehow, I knew it had been in me all along.

When it was time for the journey home, I did so with great reluctance. Like a mole hibernating in the soft, warm depths of the earth, I'd felt so safe and nurtured in this community of like-minded souls that I baulked at the thought of going back to my everyday life.

But of course I did go home and, over the coming weeks, I felt that something important had shifted in my inner world. I can see now how this is reflected in my journal: by the second week in February, I was able to record some easing of the withdrawal effects and some glimpses of light on the horizon:

> *Sleep not bad on the whole . . . Depression hardly there . . . Rational mind beginning to work! Had a slight feeling of happiness the other night – the first time I've had that feeling in years: I could weep!*

> 11 February 2013 (2.5mg Valium)

Meanwhile, I was continuing to make breakthroughs in my sessions with Lisa and benefiting more deeply from my yoga practice:

> *I am learning about personal boundaries . . . Learning that the pattern of abuse [from my earliest days] has been replicating itself throughout my adult life, in my relation-ships with men . . . I'm beginning to move out of that and to say 'no', both literally and internally too. The yoga practice, as well as therapy, is helping me to have more*

awareness . . . It's going to be a slow process, but it will save me.

Although in the interim I hit many lows, by the third week in March, when I'd cut the Valium to 1.5mg, the glimpses of something better on the horizon in my daily life were clearer and more long-lasting. I was able to record in my diary that:

My days are better . . . Mood is good. Feeling more grounded with my daily yoga practice and now meditation too . . . Had a bit of peace from my skin for a few hours last night – I wept for the relief (and the reprieve).

25 March 2013 (1.5mg Valium)

I knew that the tears of relief were a hopeful sign – evidence, at last, that after so long feeling emotionless, or suddenly in the grip of inexplicable rage or sadness, I was beginning to feel something again, and actually able to cry for positive reasons!

Suddenly, around this point – towards the end of March 2013 – it can be seen from my journal entries that something truly significant had begun to happen in my inner world. Re-reading this section, even today, more than six years later, I'm moved to tears. This is no fleeting glimpse of light; even now, it feels like the full flooding of sunlight from above, after dense clouds have shifted, bringing warmth, hope and a vital sense of the deep joy of being alive.

Looking into Buddhism is finally giving me a sense that I am finding a belief system that feels right. I have a long journey ahead but, somehow, I feel as if the journey is headed for home – to me, to the bit of me that is

211

real. Before now, I have just not known how to find my mind. But of course – I am not my thoughts! It all makes sense now. I am my mind, that is the pure, clear, natural essence that really lives. My mantra right now is 'I trust myself; I am a good person.' I return to the eternal breath; I stabilise by breathing in and breathing out. It makes me feel cloaked in warmth and love. It's me, finally.

I look forward to this journey with my body and getting to know my essence. Learning to trust that death is just my breath and my thoughts ceasing, but not me . . . Bless the day I was afforded this insight. I am going to be released from the pain of living as I let go. I've been hanging on so tightly that I have hardened to a deep cellular level. In time, I will unfold like a morning glory and see the truth as it comes to me. I belong, finally, to this energy system . . . I am at home.

Even though this was significant, the beginnings of an incredible transformation that would stay with me at a deep level for the coming weeks and indeed years, I continued with daily ups and downs for the period that followed. As I noted in my diary:

I have been trying so hard, but for every good period, I get slammed in return . . .

And now that I was beginning little by little to emerge into the world again, I was intensely aware of how low my confidence was in social situations:

My self-confidence is at an all-time low. But I'm keeping up the yoga and meditation – these are the only things

that help me feel whole and connected . . . I am craving
a community where I can grow; I'm working on uncondi-
tional acceptance and loving those around me. Struggling
slightly still, but I have faith that when this drug no
longer exerts its influence, I will be able to feel love and
connectedness for real. I must keep telling myself that I'm
a good person and that I am lovable.

1 May 2013

By 10 May, I'd managed to reduce my daily Valium dose to just 0.5mg – and I was very much aware that the end date for my final taper was at last in sight. However, I also knew that it was at exactly this point the first time around that the seizures had returned, and it wasn't easy to keep at bay my fear that it would happen again. There was also a more general anxiety about how I would cope without any Valium in my system:

Looking forward to being benzo-free on about 31 [May].
I'm very apprehensive as to how my body will respond to
being without the drug . . .

10 May 2013

Yet I knew, from the *Ashton Manual*, that this worry is extremely common for many people at this stage in the process – but also that these anxieties are mainly of a psychological nature, rather than being directly related to physical dependency, since by this time, thanks to the steady tapering programme, my body had had plenty of time to get used to compensating for the reduction in the drug. So as long as I could remain seizure-free, I knew that now it was a matter of just holding my nerve and keeping my faith in the process and, most of all, in myself.

On 27 May 2013, I did the final taper, jumping from 0.25mgs of Valium to nothing. In so many ways, it felt like jumping off a cliff not knowing if there was a safety net. It felt momentous – a leap of faith into the free-floating space of the rest of my life. I knew that, in many ways, another journey was beginning, one that would also require effort, learning and faith. But I also knew that I had been through hell – the worst hell of all, that of my own mind – and I had survived. I was determined to make every single moment of the rest of my life worth the pain and suffering, and to follow the deep longing, which had always been in me, finally to embrace something far better.

Twenty-Seven

May 2013

Dear Friends

I wish to share with you, my fellow journeyers, that as of 27 May 2013, I am free of Valium, finally. I began in severe tolerance, had one bad attempt at tapering Clobazam, had one very difficult crossover to Valium, followed by one fourteen-month taper, had a seizure at 0.5mg, reinstated Valium on doctor's advice and took another nine-month taper, and now I'm finally at my destination zero. I didn't say anything, as I wanted to be sure I could get through the first week without seizures – and so far, so good!

I'm not sure what to expect from here but I can report that, right now, I feel almost completely normal. Only the nights can still be a bit challenging but are very manageable at the same time, for the most part. I've had the most horrendous two and a half years with never a let-up, ever, and I must admit to being brought to my knees – physically and especially mentally. At many times in my life to this point, I have been faced with some very traumatic events, but withdrawal took the show for horror. And that is saying something, believe me!

For me, things only began to get better at 0.5mg. The depersonalisation/derealisation and depression began to lift and I no longer wished that I was dead every day, and instead of being hemmed in my own private mental prison something on the horizon began to open up. And when the morning finally dawned where I found myself feeling glad to be alive, I wept with relief. My inner world has been such a barren landscape for so many years that to not be feeling like a Martian and everyone else Earthlings has been like a rebirth. I still have some adjusting to do but, to be honest, it's not so much. Once we are on the path to recovery, we begin to naturally gather momentum, and we can pick up the pieces quite quickly.

I have changed in this period, and I can truly say that it's for the better. I have a different set of boundaries now, and my ability to understand myself and to express myself is much more mature. I realise that not everything is as we see it. I'm much calmer and I'm living in the here-and-now instead of rushing. I only have today, and that's just fine. I hope that I will never forget this experience and what it's taught me because, as horrific as it has been, I know I have grown immensely through it.

I'm very much aware that I will have peaks and troughs as I wind my way to recovery, but I'm okay with that. The taper is over and I'm on the next part of this journey now.

My wish in writing this is to offer some light and hope to all who are still having a hard time. I never thought that I would be writing this 'freedom post' with such a light heart. As far as I was concerned, I was damaged goods, someone who would only ever be able to eke out an existence for the rest of my days, and just somehow cope with how I was. But that is not how it has turned out after all, and now I can see that it really is the passage of time that is the healer in benzo withdrawal. Time and more time, just as much time as each of us needs.

With much warmth and love to all

Rachel

This was the 'freedom letter' that I published on Benzo Buddies just over a week after I took my last Valium dose.

The two and a half years it took to get there I can only describe as absolute living hell.

Yet even as I write those words – 'absolute living hell' – I find myself smiling. Of course, there's very little intrinsically funny about the protracted and painful process of coming off a powerful psychotropic drug, but even before then my life had hardly been a bed of roses. At times, the sheer accumulation of traumas really does strike me as absurd, almost farcical. I doubt I would have survived as well if it wasn't for my sense of humour, as dark as it can be at times.

Given all that I'd been through, it might be difficult to understand why I describe the period coming off prescription drugs as one of the most painful in my life. The truth is that this particular experience was different from the other traumas in important ways. Throughout so much of what had happened – the grief of bereavement, the pain of raising a daughter whose father died before she was born, the fear that comes with life-or-death surgery, paralysis, trauma – I was still my own person. As best I could, I tried to get on in life by drawing on the bedrock of my character, discovering in the process a strength I hadn't known was there, but which I'd simply had to develop as a child in order to survive the toxic environment in which I grew up. When it came to grief, I learned to trust the process and have faith that, somehow, I had the resources to live through it. And when it came to my illness, I had to face down the prospect of my own death, and then find within myself the will to push the limits of my recovery as far as I could. In all of this, I retained some idea of who I was and some sense of personal dignity.

In all of these experiences, I had some understanding of what was happening. And while my responses might have been extreme and, at times, very painful to experience, to my mind, they fell within the boundaries of 'normal' (whatever that is). The grief, the fear, the sadness, the desolation – all these were to be expected as I reacted to the blows life dealt me. But the experience of coming off drugs was the first time my own mind completely turned against me. I simply lost all sense of myself. At times, I quite literally felt insane, and certainly there was no real sense of hope, only the will to survive. In many ways there is nothing more cruel or painful to live through. There is a very particular kind of devastation that hits you when your own mind can no longer be relied on, when you experience an absolute loss of identity and of any grasp on reality.

My suffering was compounded by a sense of isolation which was absolute and unremitting. Through all of my other experiences, my family and friends and wider acquaintances tried to be there for me. They did the very best they could, in the knowledge that what I was suffering had a real, easily identifiable cause. But when everything spiralled completely out of my control and I literally did lose my mind, many of those who'd been so supportive over the years simply fell away. It was mooted that I was mentally unstable – that my tough life had tipped me into emotional instability and that I might never get better. That's when most people jumped ship and I was left truly alone. If it hadn't been for my mother and the professionals I paid to support me, apart from the odd visit from a friend, I would have been almost completely without human contact during those two and a half years. It was the loneliest, most isolating time in my life. I would not wish it on anyone.

It would take another few years for me to complete the process of coming off all of the anti-epilepsy drugs which had been part of my daily existence for years since my surgery in 2006. I had been on and off so many prescribed medications over the years and to my mind it was time to take stock; I desperately wanted to know if any real healing had happened over the years, or if my brain was as scarred and damaged as was first thought. I did this very cautiously, beginning by reducing one drug at a time, using micro reductions. My time withdrawing from Valium had taught me that these medications needed to be respected so I proceeded cautiously, very slowly stealing micro amounts from my daily dose, one drug at a time with gaps of six months between each different withdrawal. My doctor at the time was dubious as to whether or not I still had the crippling seizures that surgery had left me with, but I told her I was determined to follow my plan through and assured her that I would take one hundred per cent of the responsibility if things went wrong. The fear, of course, was that my seizures would return, with possible devastating consequences, since the doctors were convinced that it was only my drug regimen that was keeping them at bay. And of course, the prospect of their return was far more terrifying to me than it was to them; only I, and anyone who has experienced such things, can be fully aware of how frightening and debilitating they can be.

But even though I was now free of benzos and had experienced such a marked shift for the better in my inner world and in the quality of my everyday life, I absolutely believed that the stultifying cocktail of other anti-epileptic drugs was still preventing me from feeling, rendering me a diluted version of who I really was. I knew there had to be more than this to life, and that if I didn't at least try to see what life would be like without this numbing cocktail of chemicals, I would spend the rest of my days wondering about what might have been.

Because I wasn't physically dependent on the other drugs in the way I had been on the benzos, the process of weaning myself off them was in some senses a little less physically arduous. Still, it was a long, hard slog, and again I was subject to some miserable withdrawal symptoms. I had indescribable attacks of rage and the most intractable insomnia as I came off Tegretol and had to battle the ongoing fear that my seizures would return. But, miraculously, they didn't. I couldn't believe my luck, and every day I was more and more encouraged as I had first one week and then a month seizure free. The feeling was unbelievable. Was this possible, was I home and dry? Could I continue to live medication free and hold on to this feeling of clarity and joy? It seemed so, and the tears that fell had a completely different flavour now. It appeared that I had made it! I continued my regular yoga/meditation practice and attended therapy throughout this time, and was very much aware that, every day, I was only taking baby steps into unknown territory – not only in allowing my body to adjust after so many years of reliance on medication but also in terms of re-entering 'normal' life. I had spent so many years in enforced isolation that I had taken on behaviours that were not dissimilar to those of a person who had become institutionalised. I was beginning again, quite literally. In the early stages of this re-entering process, I felt emotionally raw, insecure and very gauche in any social setting. I marvelled at others' apparent ease with routine occurrences such as chatting to a neighbour in the street. I observed with intense curiosity and began committing to memory the body language used, the lilt and tone of someone who hadn't, to all intents and purposes, been effectively imprisoned for so many years. Outside of this reintegration, I was consolidating in myself a radically different way of being in the world – one of awareness, gratitude and contentment. I was content just to be alive; the world seemed shiny and new and I was delighted as each day dawned and I'd recovered some more. I knew I was forever changed, and I celebrated this. Goodness, I was beginning to like who I was becoming. I was being given yet another chance at 'doing' life and I promised myself that I would never forget that to be alive is truly a miracle.

By 2015, I had come through the worst of my recovery and was able, finally, to say I was living completely drug-free. There had been a huge opening up in my inner world, which naturally happened at its own pace as I continued my spiritual practice and read voraciously; books about the real secret to living – cultivating a deeper relationship with one's self and seeking to find out who each of us is, really, just as the great teachers seek to do via their never-ending existential ponderings. I was on a journey of personal discovery, I was excited, and because of my experiences I was never going back. I became convinced that life's true riches come from the jewels inside us; we just need to choose stillness and go within. By late 2015 I was beginning to feel that it was time for me to really put myself out into the world again, as an adult woman; to work, to earn a living, to give back.

I was in a new relationship, I had moved across the country and my beautiful daughter was beginning a new adventure of her own, heading to study abroad. I had gained some confidence and was now ready for much more. From an early age I had known I was a natural carer and that I longed to serve others.

Now, because of my life's journey, I felt that I had a lot to give back, so I began looking for a therapy niche that I felt would reflect who I had become and my beliefs about humans and the amazing abilities we have to heal ourselves and our lives. It was about then that I was reintroduced to hypnotherapy through a conversation with Lauraine. She'd mentioned that she had come across a clinical hypnotherapist called Marisa Peer on YouTube and that she spoke about the power of the subconscious mind and its therapeutic potential. I took a look and, immediately, it was like a light coming on – I was able to instantly recognise that in my own clumsy and unformed way I had been intuitively harnessing the power of my own mind to heal. Once I did some more investigation, it became clear I had found the exact therapy I'd been seeking. To add to my enthusiasm, I was able to recall that I was not a complete stranger to hypnosis at all and had in fact previously used clinical hypnotherapy to overcome a terrible fear of general anaesthetics in 2005. As a little girl, I'd harboured a crippling terror of any medical procedure that warranted an anaesthetic and, consequently, I had gone to very extreme lengths to make sure I avoided ever 'being put asleep', and then, to my horror, in the autumn of 2005 I literally came face to face with that fear. To be able to have the life-saving surgery I needed I had to be cured of my phobia, and it was, I remembered then, clinical hypnotherapy that cured me completely of this visceral fear, and I was able to face surgery with far less trepidation than before.

It was all coming together! I suppose my advent into training as a therapist was a culmination of many factors: it was partly because of my earlier positive result with hypnotherapy; it was most certainly because of my recovery from my own traumatic experiences; it was, in part, because of what I'd learned about healing my own mind and body; it was because I absolutely believed in our own ability as humans to heal; it was the memory of having felt purposeful when I helped mentor Sophie and other patients in the BIRU; and likely many more facets that planted the very earliest of seeds that I could still help and serve others, not despite my own physical and emotional difficulties but because of them. And looking back to Dominic, and my time with him, I can see that caring was in my soul from those earliest of days. I was born with a will to help others, and it was a foregone conclusion that, somehow, someday, I would find my way into working formally as a therapist, and it was likely that watching that YouTube clip gave me that final push to begin to make the first formal moves that precipitated the first leg of my journey to becoming a clinical hypnotherapist, and then later to work as a life coach and keynote speaker.

Clinical hypnotherapy is neuroplasticity in therapy form and, to my mind, is exactly the direction in which therapy should be headed. Neuroplasticity is the science behind the brain's ability to heal itself. It was once thought that the brain, once matured, was fixed and that there was little that could be done for people, like me, who suffered neurological accidents, such as strokes and paralysis. However, more recent advances in medicine have brought new discoveries and an understanding that the human brain is in fact plastic, that it can heal, and that we can grow new neural pathways, which, in effect, means that we can purposefully heal from many conditions by harnessing the power of the mind and the brain to form new neural circuits. My own recovery is the living proof of this neuroplasticity and completely underpins my fascination with this whole area of therapy, which purposefully utilises the power of the subconscious mind to heal both physical and emotional issues.

Life was taking on a whole new colour, and I quickly began to realise that I had a unique ability to effect positive change in my clients. My deeper life experiences gave me a special and unique connection to my clients, and my belief that I was part of a greater energetic field that intuitively seeks alignment allowed me to step out of my own way and work with intuition and absolute trust that each client has within them the ability to heal themselves. All they need is a therapeutic nudge to guide them through the process of harnessing the power of their minds. Fascinated and humbled at the same time, I began to design other aspects of my business to further help clients live their best life. It felt like a win-win, and I grew and learned from each client and still do to this day.

In the early days, my new relationship, which had begun in mid-2013, was both a source of great joy and a cause for much anxiety. Was it the right time to be grappling with something else new? Sure, I was making great strides in my recovery, yet because my brain was finally unfettered enough to allow me to complete the very much delayed grieving process, I was also working through a lingering sense of low self-esteem as well as finally processing all the losses I had suffered. It was no surprise, then, that in my mid-forties I still had much to learn about myself and about relationships of the heart. It was like starting over again as a teenager. I was crippled with self-doubt – doubt about my looks, whether I was interesting enough, sexy enough. You name the insecurity, I had it, but still I threw myself headlong into it. In those early days I veered wildly between wanting to run away from the relationship and clinging to it like a limpet. I was all over the place. My only 'real' relationship up to this point had ended in catastrophic loss and extreme vulnerability. My new partner, Malcolm, hadn't been in any really committed long-term relationship, and by his fifties hadn't lived full-time with any of his previous loves. So our learning curves were steep. Yes, it was challenging, and, yes, it was rough at times, particularly once we spent real time together, without the heady heights of the early days. Remember, it was as if I had come out of an emotional time capsule. Everything felt like I was doing it for the first time, even sex.

So how did this experiment go? Often badly. I think the thing that kept us going was that we intrinsically really liked each other. We weathered many relationship storms and there were times when we both wanted to throw in the towel, but something drove us to keep trying. At times I thought to myself, 'I don't remember it being this difficult to love Nic', and my mind would go back to what, in my memory at least, was a familiar safety. But, together, we stuck it out. Malcolm began to adjust to me moving to live with him after Nicola left for Costa Rica; I began to trust that he wouldn't die if I couldn't see him. Malcolm began to learn to share his space; I began to believe that I was worthy of staying around for. Somehow, we bumbled our way forward and began to shape our relationship into something really workable and sustainable. We are both now much more forgiving of each other. We have grown close and he is my best friend. We share great times, are deeply caring of each other, laugh madly at things that others mightn't appreciate, strive to spend time together outdoors and share a deep concern for our beautiful planet. In a nutshell, I found love again, and I feel blessed.

In the years since, I have continued to recover. In the early days of our relationship, I was unable to walk on uneven ground or climb over a gate, and I was continually dropping things. My words would often come out as complete gibberish, my memory was shaky, and I had little use of my left hand. I was also much quieter, more vulnerable, I'd say. I was quite a handful, really, and Malcolm never faltered in his care for me. I think the biggest challenge came when I began to regain my faculties as I stripped the last of the drugs from my life one by one. I began to emerge as an autonomous woman. I stopped dropping things, my memory improved, I gained more use of my left hand. I was making huge strides forwards and, perhaps understandably, Malcolm was beginning to wonder who I was now. When we met, I was a little dependent and not so strong, and he could see the strength I now had emerging quickly. No wonder he took some time to adjust to the healed me. The woman I was growing into was so different – so much more independent, confident and energetic – from the Rachel he had first met! We talked about this recently and, in his quiet way, he let me know that at first he didn't know if he liked the new emerging me. He kind of liked the woman he met originally, and yet he knew he had to adjust to this new version.

Looking back, I can see how difficult that might have been for him, but of course I had no real idea of the contrast between the old me and the new me. This emerging me was unfolding like a butterfly from a chrysalis. There was no going back. The good news is that we are through this transition and now find, to our delight, that we have both adjusted. Our relationship has a more mature footing and we are content in our shared lives. Malcolm continues to tell me how proud he is of my achievements and how he admires the work I do now.

Health wise, I am nearly fully recovered. Emotionally, I'm better than I've ever been. Each day I purposefully cultivate an inner joy and contentment, and this gives me a huge sense of well-being. I still have some residual loss of function in my left hand and arm, but over the years I've grown used to it. I can do most things; I just have no dexterity or fine motor skills in my left hand, but I'm completely happy with that and always say to myself that it's good enough. I have good enough use of it, and, besides, I have retrained myself to be right-handed and have no intention of trying to push it by trying to rewire things in the reverse; it might take a while! I still experience some physical symptoms, mainly from the benzo withdrawal. It's not much, but it's enough to remind me that I have quite a story behind me. I still get brain 'zaps' from time to time, and at night I can still get little bolts of electrical shock up through my feet and long bouts of insomnia. This is all cyclical, and while at times it can be a bit distressing, to be honest, I am so very happy just to be here and to live with such joy and contentment that I hardly dwell on these last few symptoms because, in comparison to how things were before, they are small fry. I'm good at honouring where I am at any particular time and manage my energy accordingly. What I say these days is 'thank you, life'!

Nicola surprised (why am I surprised!) and amazed me when, at sixteen, she decided she wanted to go to a United World College in Costa Rica to finish her high-schooling. I couldn't believe it, as she had long been plagued with crippling separation anxiety which stemmed from our time in Trieste. She had found it difficult to let me out of her sight. This was understandable, given the terrifying experiences she had had to endure, first with my illness, and then living the chaotic and unstable life I gave her as I erratically chopped and changed her life on a whim. Looking back, I'm surprised that she weathered this instability so well and that it was only this one issue that outwardly affected her life. My heart breaks even now to imagine her loneliness as I constantly moved us around. I was completely unaware of the consequences for this gorgeous girl who loved me so dearly and yet who feared that I would one night get up and leave her behind. It seems implausible to me, but to Nicola, she feared I would leave and never return. Even the idea of this now makes me angry at the selfishness the drugs had engendered in me. Rarely do I look back with anything but love and gratitude for my life, but the fear and suffering I caused Nicola will always weigh heavily in my heart.

So, imagine my astonishment at her choosing to go right across the world (did she learn this from me?). My immediate response was, 'But you are only just finding your strength and settling into school here, how about UWC Wales, it's closer.' Her response was, 'I want to go to Costa Rica because the surf is good.' So that is what she did. I cannot properly describe the pride I felt as we saw her off at Dublin, bound for New York and then on to San José, Costa Rica, aged sixteen. The UWC turned out to be a wonderful move for Nicola, and my fears that she wouldn't manage without me were unfounded. She thrived. I must have done something right at some point as a parent to have restored her confidence to such a degree.

Today, entering my sixth decade, I look back and find I am full of gratitude, not necessarily because I'm still alive, but more because my inner world is mostly that of resonance and alignment. I no longer feel the weight of shame and guilt that I carried throughout my life – from my earliest childhood, in fact. That burden is gone and the voices in my head today are those of gentleness and praise. This, to me, is the biggest celebration; finally, I am free to live consciously and it's up to me what I populate my inner world with. I feel proud of having got this far. I love being a woman in my fifties. I'm content and joyous about my life and curious about the vast possibilities open to me in the future.

People still ask me how I managed to live through so much tragedy and reach the point I am at now in life – deeply appreciative for every day I live, content with what I have, happy to be alive and excited at the prospect of the future. Not for one moment do I assume that I will never experience more sadness or trauma, or that life will never throw something apparently insurmountable in my path again. I know that, in the broadest sense, the future is uncertain for me, as it is for all of us. And perhaps some small part of me can't help anticipating the next trauma or tragedy. But what

I have learned, through everything, is that these experiences are as much a part of life as the happy, joyful times.

I'm no longer waiting for something better, holding out for the good times and wishing away the present. I'm focused on what is happening here and now and, at my core, I hold the knowledge that no matter what happens, I will cope with it with bravery. At last I have confidence in my true self and in the certainty that life goes on. I also know that it is when the storm is at its height and things are most turbulent that I can feel most viscerally alive. And I am convinced that we all have this thread of steel – this will to overcome and to survive – running through us like a spine.

Twenty-Eight

Not so long ago – just a few months back, in fact – I found myself in a situation which brought long-forgotten feelings flooding back – feelings of being pushed to my limits and of being in mortal danger. It was a very graphic, powerful reminder of those times in my life when all I could do was persist, put my head down and hope to get through the next moment, the next hour, the next day. And, as usual, this happened when I was least expecting it.

Malcolm and I had gone on a rowing trip over a weekend – something that, as experienced rowers and lovers of the sea, we both enjoy doing in our leisure time. We planned to travel quite a distance, relatively speaking, but the weather was fine and bright, the sea was calm and the forecast for the weekend was very good. Our plan was to row to Inish Turk, an island just off the Mayo coast, have a pint in the community centre, cook over a gas stove, enjoy an overnight camp by the shore, and then row back the following day in a leisurely fashion.

Although the wind had come up a bit, we were in great form as we set off the next morning. About an hour into the row, however, conditions began to deteriorate. The wind began to pick up and dark clouds appeared in a sky that just a short time before had been clear and bright. The surface of the water was no longer calm, and soon, large, steely grey waves were slopping over the side. As experienced sailors, we were both a bit surprised; as always, we'd checked the forecast judiciously when making our preparations, and it had looked as if conditions would be fine for the weekend, with nothing to cause concern in the tides or weather fronts. But we also knew that the sea is never entirely predictable and that things can turn around very quickly.

We were far out at sea by this point and were both aware that the nearest land, even in calm conditions, was a good hour's row away. So we kept our heads down and began to ramp up our rowing efforts, hoping that the squall would pass quickly and the waves would die back again. But it didn't happen. Instead, the storm set in, in earnest this time. The sky darkened and the wind began to really gather momentum. As we kept rowing, the waves became bigger and bigger, pitching over the side in rapid succession and more forcefully with every minute that passed. Soon it felt like we were entirely at their mercy, with the small craft lurching between deep troughs, as a wall of water rose above us and the wave reached its full height, and we were pitched up and thrown high onto the wave's crest. In spite of our joint experience of the sea and without a word being exchanged, we were both a little fearful now about the situation we were in and about what would happen if we didn't make land as soon as possible.

As we kept rowing with every ounce of strength we had, I felt something in me shift. It was as if a switch had been flicked and my mind had moved into another mode, a different place – one I recognised from long ago. All my focus, all my attention, was narrowed down and channelled into the absolutely essential things we needed to do to ensure that we kept afloat and, ultimately, made land. There was only the physical rhythm of rowing – 'oar in, oar out'; the short, urgent exchanges of encouragement; the channelling of all physical energy to the task at hand. At the same time, my thought processes, my rational thinking abilities, took on a heightened sense of clarity, a greater economy and speed, as

I assessed our rapidly evolving circumstances and calculated how we could best try to direct the boat to maximise our chances of reaching land quickly.

I believe that this ability to shift gears is a switch we all have, something we can all access when our basic survival instincts kick in. In the same way animals in the wild can, when our lives are under threat we can very quickly apprehend the source of danger in a situation and identify what actions we need to take to have the best chances of escaping intact.

And so, Malcolm and I naturally fell into a physical rhythm as we rowed – 'oar in, oar out' – and began to count aloud to mark the strokes: 'One – two – three – four – five' and again, 'One – two – three – four – five', alternating between five strong, powerful strokes and five lighter strokes, again and again. In doing so, we were intuitively creating a mantra that would enable intense focus on the task at hand, with no room for any other thoughts or distractions. We had created our own mental zone, a place where there was an absolute economy of physical effort and mental output, ensuring that we conserved our resources and expended only the energy that was absolutely necessary.

As the sea began to roll and the wind picked up further, we found ourselves continually having to row into the wind in order to make any progress towards land, and to avoid being driven further out to sea. In a sense, this was counterintuitive, since it meant we were rowing in what seemed like the wrong direction – against the wind – although the nearest land was actually downwind, oblique to us. Yet somehow, we were both able to make the calculation very swiftly that that was what we had to do in that situation. Meanwhile, I had a growing realisation that it was going to take a long time to extricate ourselves from the danger we faced, and that we'd need to summon huge reserves of physical strength and stamina to be able to keep going for as long as we needed to. I knew that it was already at least two hours since the bad weather had set in, and that it might take a few more hours of concerted, unflagging rowing effort to ensure we got to safety.

But as fatigue began to take hold, I was somehow able to access reserves of strength that I hadn't imagined I possessed. And as we continued to chant our mantra to keep time, I felt that exhaustion was giving way to a sense of exhilaration – what I can only describe as a sheer, unadulterated joy in the rhythm of physical effort and in the uncharted mental space I was now occupying so fully and unreservedly. Alongside this, I was filled with a deep-seated certainty that I had the absolute wherewithal to see us through this situation and ensure a safe landing.

We must have rowed for a good four and a half hours before finally, unbelievably, we managed to reach land and rest our tired limbs. Only as we climbed out of the boat, with legs trembling from sheer effort, did I notice that I had lost all the skin on the palm of my hands (from contact with the oars), my buttocks felt bruised and raw and my bare feet were aching from having been pushed so hard and for so long into the bottom of the boat. Only then could I allow the complete physical exhaustion and muscle weakness to wash over me, as we wobbled up the shore from the boat and embraced each other, smiling with relief.

Lundy; Fastnet; Irish Sea; Shannon; Rockall; Malin; Hebrides; Bailey; Fair Isle; Faeroes; Southeast Iceland . . .

Epilogue

Today Nicola is in her early twenties and is an amazing woman, studying linguistics at University College London and thriving. I often look to her for wisdom these days. She is so alive – a free spirit who is immensely passionate about travel and loves to see as much of the world as she can. We have a remarkable relationship and I am in awe of her groundedness and her ability to find joy in everything she does. I love to hear her say, 'That was the best day ever', and she says that a lot. I learn every day from her.

Lauraine became the sister I never had. Today she lives in West Cork with her husband, Tim, and their grown-up daughter, Tara. Lauraine went on to establish an interior design business and is passionate about her work. We speak at least three times a week.

Breeda and I remain very close friends. She has continued to flourish in her own life and career, successfully pursuing her own passions and purpose as a singer and songwriter with the most beautiful voice. She released her own album in late 2019. Her work is so heart-centred and so worth hearing – true solace for the soul (www.breedamurphy.com).

Jane Gotto continues to work as a psychotherapist and lives in Taunton, Somerset, with her husband, Lars. They have one grown-up daughter, Lotta. I remain close both to Jane and her twin sister, Sara.

My beloved cowboy boots are still in my wardrobe – a bit battered-looking now – and whenever I look at them I get a lump in my throat; they will always be a reminder of just how far I've come.

And finally, I'm happy to say that my beloved mother, Shirley Bendon, is alive and well at eighty-five and these days spends most of her time painting in her sun-filled conservatory. I visit her often and we are very close.

ACKNOWLEDGEMENTS

My first thanks must go to the two most important women in this story – to my daughter, Nicola, and my mother.

Nicola, you kept me going and you were my reason for fighting so hard. Thank you for continuing to love me, regardless of everything I've put you through. You are a shining light in the world, and I could not be prouder of the woman you have become, despite my shady parenting!

My beloved mother, I cannot thank you enough for your tireless support of me in the long years it took. You had your own losses and pain to shoulder and yet that did not stop your never-ending supply of love. Your constant mantra that, one day, I would live with joy and contentment kept me going, even in my darkest of days.

Emily and Hayley, your father loved you both so dearly and would have been so immensely proud of the wonderful women you have become today.

Malcolm, thank you for your belief in me and for supporting me so fully in getting my story out to the world.

To my family of origin, without your love and support throughout my most difficult of challenges, I might not have made it. Thank you, Mel, Nicky and Adrian, and your respective wives, Jane, Jan and Naomi, and your families. Each of you in your own way, quite literally, kept my head above water when I was sinking, and I also have so much gratitude for the love and support that you and your families gave Nicola when I was not able.

To Nic's family: I am blessed to have you all in my life. Jane, Lars, Sara, Chris and Clare, and your amazing families, I offer you the very same deepest love and thanks. You took up the mantle when Nic died and never left my side, and it's been your love and support also that kept me going through the tough times.

Many blessings to you, Jane Gotto, for introducing me to Ken Zilkha.

So many wonderful people have helped me on my recovery journey and I would wish to acknowledge you all here: however, this list is not exhaustive, and if I leave anyone out, it is purely an oversight and in no way intentional.

My heartfelt thanks go to Lauraine and Tim Farley, Breeda Murphy, Raushana and John Wickett, Arianne and Robert Boon, Shona Jackson, Sally Barnes, Eve and Stuart Fuller, Anne Smith, Reverend Richard Henderson, Reverend Chris Peters, Heidi Krug-Wischniewski, Jenny Jardin, Colin Barnes, Helen Quirke, Zeik and Margaret Tuit, Claudia and Michael Kinmonth, Philippe Collignon, the scuba diving communities, both in Ireland and England, Richard Nelson, Ken Zilkha, Andrew Molyneaux, the Frenchay Hospital, BIRU, Richard Martin, John Lucey, Peter Kiniorons, Jacky and Tim Zilkha, Benzobuddies, Flip, Margot, Pianogirl, Siobhan O'Callaghan, Wayne Santry, Geri McGeoghan Santry, Christina and Bartosz Stentoft, Lisa Brinkman, Bernie Smyth, Florence Vion, Jessica Hatchett, Stephen Gascoigne, Henry McGrath, John and Mary Kearney, Joan Dineen, Michael Dinneen, Professor Aine Burns, Michael Butrum, the Royal National Lifeboat Institute, the Irish Coast Guard, and the wider communities of Glandore, Leap and Union Hall.

Thank you to my wonderful agent, Paul Feldstein, of the Feldstein Agency: you got this book in front of the right people.

With special thanks to my incredible editors: Susan Feldstein, Gillian Fallon and Sam Boyce. Without your tireless work, this book would not be in the amazing shape it is. I am so very grateful to each of you for your expertise and professionalism, which meant this manuscript gained a finesse that would not otherwise have been there.

An additional thank you goes to the fantastic team at the Little A imprint at Amazon, especially Victoria Pepe, Sammia Hamer and Victoria Haslam.

SUPPORT NETWORKS AND FURTHER RESOURCES

Benzodiazepine Withdrawal

Professor C. Heather Ashton, *Benzodiazepines: How They Work and How to Withdraw*, aka *The Ashton Manual*, revised edition (Newcastle: Newcastle University, 2002). Available free of charge from the Benzodiazepine Information Coalition: www.benzoinfo.com/ashtonmanual

Peter R. Breggin MD, *Psychiatric Drug Withdrawal: A Guide for Prescribers, Therapists, Patients and Their Families* (New York: Springer, 2013)

Jack Hobson-Dupont, *The Benzo Book: Getting Safely Off Tranquilizers* (Essex Press, 2006)

www.benzobuddies.org: This site provided me with a sense of community that at the time was entirely absent from the rest of my life. I became a moderator and then an administrator, and also a mentor to others, and the sense of connection and satisfaction this gave me is something for which I'll forever be grateful.

YOGA

Bernie Clarke and Sarah Powers, *The Complete Guide to Yin Yoga* (Ashland, OR: White Cloud Press, 2012)

Sarah Powers, *Insight Yoga* (Boulder, CO: Shambhala, 2009)

SPIRITUAL AND PERSONAL GROWTH

The Dalai Lama, *The Art of Happiness* (London: Hodder, 1999)

Lama Dudjom Dorjee, *Heartfelt Advice* (Ithaca, NY: Snow Lion, 2010)

Thich Nhat Hanh, *The Miracle of Mindfulness* (London: Random House, 2008)

Thich Nhat Hanh, *No Death, No Fear* (London: Random House, 2002)

Eckhart Tolle, *The Power of Now* (London: Hodder, 2005)

Eckhart Tolle, *Oneness with All Life* (London: Penguin, 2018)

Oprah Winfrey, *What I Know for Sure* (London: Macmillan, 2014)

Trauma Recovery

Felicity Douglas, *A Tale of Two Dogs and a Bear: My Journey of Healing from Childhood Trauma* (Lulu.com, 2020)

Bessel van der Kolk, *The Body Keeps the Score: Mind, Brain and Body in the Transformation of Trauma* (London: Penguin, 2015)

Peter A. Levine, *Waking the Tiger: Healing Trauma* (Berkeley, CA: North Atlantic Books, 1997)

Stephen W. Porges, *The Polyvagal Theory: Neurophysiological Foundations of Emotions, Attachment, Communication and Self-Regulation* (London: Norton, 2011)

The Power of the Mind

Gil Boyne, *Self-Hypnosis* (London: Westwood Publishing, 2017)

Dr Joe Dispenza, *You Are the Placebo* (London: Hay House, 2014)

Milton H. Erickson and Sidney Rosen, *My Voice Will Go with You: The Teaching Tales of Milton H. Erickson* (New York: Norton, 1991)

Bruce H. Lipton, *The Biology of Belief* (London: Hay House, 2015)

Joseph Murphy, *The Power of Your Subconscious Mind* (Radford, VA: Wilder Publications, 2007)

Suzanne O'Sullivan, *It's All in Your Head: Stories from the Frontline of Psychosomatic Illness* (London: Random House, 2016)

INSPIRATIONAL

Edith Eger, *The Choice* (London: Random House, 2018)

Viktor E. Frankl, *Man's Search for Meaning* (London: Random House, 2004)

Kahlil Gibran, *The Prophet* (various editions)

David Sheff, *The Buddhist on Death Row* (London: HarperCollins, 2020)

GRIEF

Megan Devine, *It's OK that You're Not OK: Meeting Grief and Loss in a Culture that Doesn't Understand* (Boulder, CO: Sounds True, 2017)

Denise Riley, *Time Lived, without Its Flow* (London: Picador, 2019)

Nutrition and Lifestyle

Dr Mark Hyman, *Food: WTF Should I Eat?* (London: Yellow Kite, 2018)

Dr Mark Hyman, *The UltraMind Solution* (New York: Scribner, 2010)

Patrick Holford, *Optimum Nutrition For the Mind* (London: Piatkus, 2007)

Jason Fung and Jimmy Moore, *The Complete Guide to Fasting* (Las Vegas NV: Victory Belt, 2016)

Shane O'Mara, *In Praise of Walking* (London: Bodley Head, 2019)

ABOUT THE AUTHOR

Photo © Nicola Gotto

Rachel Gotto was born and grew up in Glandore in West Cork, a few short steps from the Atlantic Ocean. An adept boat person from an early age, and most at home on the waves, it was there she developed the tenacious spirit that later proved invaluable when faced with a litany of personal traumas and tragedies.

Having lost her closest brother as a young man to cancer, Rachel was six months pregnant with her daughter when her husband died in a tragic diving accident. Diagnosed a few years later with a life-threatening brain tumour, she underwent life-saving surgery that resulted in her becoming paralysed. What followed was a slow and painful recovery marred by a growing dependence on her prescribed medication.

Now a celebrated keynote speaker, life coach and clinical hypnotherapist, Rachel lives on the west coast of Ireland, in County Galway, where she enjoys being in nature. She loves to swim, fish, cook, read, walk, keep pet hens, and spend time with family and friends.